International praise for **NIR BARAM** and *A LAND WITHOUT BORDERS*

'Baram produced a painful, even shocking travel book. Although I do not share some of his analysis and his ultimate conclusions, I am still impressed by his sharp eye and his fierce sense of the Israeli Palestinian tragedy.' Amos Oz

'A book that is a fascinating and charged document about the meaning of home, security and freedom, on both sides of the divide.' *NRG*

'Behind the slogans and the messages, Baram exposes a measure of the multifarious world that exists among the lords of the land.' *Haaretz*

Praise for **NIR BARAM** and *GOOD PEOPLE*

'A pacey, plot-heavy novel of dramatic events and big ideas.' *Economist*

'*Good People* is a richly textured panorama of German and Russian life…This ample novel lives most memorably through Baram's vignettes of people, dwellings, cities, landscapes and the like that seem to lie, at times, at the periphery of its central concerns.' *Sydney Morning Herald*

'Precise and evocative, *Good People* is a riveting glimpse into a different place and a different time.' *Canberra Weekly*

'One of the most intriguing writers in Israeli literature today.' *Haaretz*

'A groundbreaker…Riveting reading.' *Qantas Magazine*

NIR BARAM was born into a political family in Jerusalem in 1976. His grandfather and father were both ministers in Israeli Labor Party governments. He has worked as a journalist and an editor, and as an advocate for equal rights for Palestinians. Baram began publishing fiction when he was twenty-two, and is the author of five novels, including *Good People*, which was translated into English for the first time in 2016. His novels have been translated into more than ten languages and have received critical acclaim around the world. He has been shortlisted several times for the Sapir Prize and in 2010 he received the Prime Minister's Award for Hebrew Literature.

JESSICA COHEN is a freelance translator born in England, raised in Israel, and living in Denver. She translates contemporary Israeli prose, poetry, and other creative works. Her translations include critically acclaimed works by major Israeli writers including David Grossman, Etgar Keret, Rutu Modan, Dorit Rabinyan, Ronit Matalon, Amir Gutfreund, and Tom Segev.

A LAND WITHOUT BORDERS

MY JOURNEY AROUND EAST JERUSALEM AND THE WEST BANK

NIR BARAM

TRANSLATED FROM THE HEBREW BY JESSICA COHEN

TEXT PUBLISHING MELBOURNE AUSTRALIA

textpublishing.com.au

The Text Publishing Company
Swann House, 22 William Street, Melbourne, Victoria 3000, Australia

The Text Publishing Company (UK) Ltd
130 Wood Street, London EC2V 6DL, United Kingdom

First published in Israel, 2015, in Hebrew by Am Oved as *In a Land Beyond the Mountains*
First published in English in 2017 by The Text Publishing Company

Cover design by Text
Page design by Jess Horrocks
Maps by Simon Barnard
Typeset by J&M Typesetting

Printed in Australia by Griffin Press, an Accredited ISO AS/NZS 14001:2004 Environmental Management System printer.

9781925355222 (Australian paperback)
9781911231080 (UK paperback)
9781922253804 (ebook)

National Library of Australia Cataloguing-in-Publication entry
Creator: Baram, Nir, author.
Title: A land without borders : my journey around East Jerusalem and the West Bank / by Nir Baram; translated from the Hebrew by Jessica Cohen.
Subjects: Arab-Israeli conflict. Jerusalem—Ethnic relations. Jerusalem—Description and travel. West Bank—Ethnic relations. West Bank—Description and travel.
Other Creators/Contributors: Cohen, Jessica, translator.
Dewey Number: 956.94

A LAND WITHOUT BORDERS

Mediterranean Sea

Haifa •

Nazareth •

Tel Aviv •

WEST BANK

JERUSALEM •

Dead Sea

GAZA STRIP

• Be'er Sheva

ISRAEL

EGYPT

Eilat •

East Jerusalem

Armistice Demarcation
(Green Line)

West Jerusalem

SYRIA

IRAQ

ISRAEL
AND ENVIRONS

JORDAN

SAUDI ARABIA

0 10 20 30 40 50 60km

0   10   20   30   40mi

CONTENTS

You Must Learn How to Listen to the Land

In 2014 I decided to travel the length of the Green Line, the demarcation line agreed in the 1949 armistice agreements between Israel and its neighbors. On the other side of the Green Line is the West Bank, which Israel has now occupied for fifty years, ever since the Six-Day War in 1967. I spent some time in East Jerusalem, too, which Israel has also occupied since 1967. I set off on this journey because I wanted to learn what this place really looks like—this part of the world where I have lived all my life and where (if all goes according to plan) I will live out the rest of my days.

Starting at a very early age, all of us have been bombarded with pictures, maps and news reports about the Israeli–Palestinian conflict. We learned about injustices, wrongdoings, even killings—whether in Jenin, at the Kalandia checkpoint, or at a demonstration near Ramallah. And our immediate response was one of horror. Sometimes, in fact, it seems we've spent most of our lives being horrified. And yet over the past few years Israelis have started to appear fatigued by their horror and its familiar companion: their sense of helplessness. Or is it that they have tired of the horror because of the helplessness? Either way, they've lost interest in the Palestinians. Most Israelis, and perhaps most people around the world, have concluded that there is no chance of resolving the conflict.

The horror, the indifference and the despair have become shopworn. It's all been said before. But the incredible thing is that the vast majority of Israelis—as well as most international spectators—know next to nothing about life on the West Bank, the area at the heart of the conflict they have spent their adult lives dissecting. Most Israelis have never visited the occupied territories, unless they were there as part of their military service, and so the debate revolves around a theoretical, ill-defined area sketched out in our political imagination, no less abstract than Syria or the Congo or so many other war-torn lands.

What has become clear in recent years is that very few of us have a comprehensive, accurate picture of the West Bank or the Green Line. This journey was my effort to examine, as frankly as possible, the connection between my own political views and the West Bank reality. I'd grown weary of the café discussions and the conferences at universities or in Geneva, where participants deliberate the finer points of the occupation without knowing where the Green Line actually runs, what a refugee camp looks like, how many people live in the Shomron settlement outposts, or where the separation wall cuts through Bethlehem.

I was driven by a personal motivation, too. Since the age of twenty-one, I have been writing newspaper articles, organizing demonstrations, signing petitions, giving speeches at rallies against the occupation and in support of the traditional two-state solution that aims to resolve the outcomes of the 1967 war. But I had an increasing sense of discomfort: was it possible that although we kept on saying the same things, the West Bank had in fact become a different place? Moreover, as I began to suspect based on what I was hearing from the Palestinians I met, had the issues themselves shifted? I could not help questioning my own positions: were the plans I was advocating implementable anymore? Were we truly acknowledging the core of the conflict? The doubts continued to nag, and I decided I needed to visit the occupied territories. In order to stand on solid political ground—as I felt I had done for many years—and voice an honest perspective, I knew I had to go and see for myself.

During the eighteen months I spent traveling around the West Bank, I would often come back to Tel Aviv and tell my friends about the things I'd seen. Their reactions ranged from surprise to disbelief. Are there really neighborhoods, like Ras Khamis in East Jerusalem, where Israeli residents live on the Palestinian side of the wall? Do these tenuous, fluid, lawless areas really exist, places with no clear municipal or national governance? Are the settlements truly spread out all over the West Bank and not only in the settlement blocs? Do Palestinians and settlers take the same roads and get stuck in the same traffic jams? Are there so many secular settlers? I gradually came to understand that the Israel I know is separated from the West Bank not only by checkpoints like Kalandia, but also—and more significantly—by a cognitive barrier, which is growing higher all the time.

I grew up in Israel in the 1980s, when hundreds of thousands of Palestinians from the West Bank worked in Israel and shared the streets of Jerusalem, Tel Aviv and Haifa with us every day. Since the Oslo Accords of the 1990s, and with greater vigor after the Second Intifada broke out in 2000 and the Israeli government built its "security fence" (the separation wall that runs along the Green Line in some sections, but mostly sits deep in the West Bank), separation between West Bank Palestinians and Israelis became more rigid, more planned. As a result, the Palestinians ostensibly disappeared from our streets and most Israelis stopped going over the Green Line. Many Jewish teenagers I spoke with have never met a Palestinian in their lives—not even one!—while Palestinian kids eyed me curiously because I was the first Jew they'd ever met. But even older Israelis, who used to maintain both working and personal relationships with Palestinians from the West Bank, have not seen one for many years.

In fact, for most Israelis the West Bank has become a domain that exists somewhere out there beyond the tall mountains, far from sight. They know that certain events occur there, they sometimes talk about the occupation and the settlements, but they have no inkling what the West Bank looks like today or how its inhabitants conduct their lives. Most Israelis who engage in political debates about the occupation are seeing, in their mind's eye, a map that is circa mid-1990s or early 2000s and therefore wholly unrelated to the changing reality on the ground. The inevitable result is that public discourse in Israel is replete with a multitude of "zombie terms" that fill the media but which turn out, if one drives West Bank roads, visits settlements and refugee camps, and stands at checkpoints, to have no bearing on reality. It's difficult to talk about a solution when you have no idea what the problem you are discussing looks like.

Undoubtedly, the geographical expanse is a topic of critical importance. But what about the human element? We all purport to speak on behalf of large groups of people; we imagine we know the Palestinians' political goals without comprehending Palestinian society's various classes and factions. We think all the settlers are obeying extremist rabbis' orders because we've seen them on television, and we assume that figures like Abu Mazen, president of the Palestinian National Authority, or the heads of Hamas or the settler leaders—a few dozen faces, in all—truly represent the millions who live in the West Bank. We like to quote commentators who confirm our opinions, and we invoke characters we have never met but who represent stereotypes we find palatable. In the course of 2014 and 2015, I spoke with hundreds of people, Jewish and Arab, from all classes and political affiliations. I listened to them, asked questions, invited them to describe their lives, their aspirations, their goals for the future.

I met them in their homes, at their workplaces, at checkpoints, on roads, in their natural habitats, and I tried to perceive their hardships at eye-level.

Sometimes I listened to people I had always viewed as political enemies—Hamas members or outpost settlers—and I got to know the stories they believe in and their plans for the future. I came to realize that the familiar division between peace-lovers and warmongers is over-simplified and unhelpful, because in fact the intricate reality that has evolved in the West Bank cannot be understood merely by answering the question "Two states: yes or no?" This reality comprises different perceptions of time and space, divergent understandings of history's formative events, religious consciousness, fears of the other, daily customs, tribulations, and ideologies. Listening to people helps formulate a more complex picture of the world, one that is often full of contradictions, but it also enables us to talk about the future in a less entrenched manner, to genuinely examine different ideas, and, above all, to understand the connection between one's political viewpoint and the reality on the ground. More than once I felt my own political positions being challenged, which forced me to acknowledge that I tend to cling to my own fixed views. "You must learn how to listen to the land," a young Palestinian from Balata Refugee Camp told me, "and I mean really listen."

Listen to the land. I pondered the meaning of his words. In his fascinating book *Palestinian Walks*, author and lawyer Raja Shehadeh quotes William Makepeace Thackeray, who traveled the West Bank in the first half of the nineteenth century and recounted his impressions in *Notes of a Journey from Cornhill to Grand Cairo*: "Fear and blood, crime and punishment, follow from page to page in frightful succession. There is not a spot at which you look, but some violent deed has been done there: some massacre has been committed, some victim has been murdered, some idol has been worshipped with bloody and dreadful rites." Thackeray's words ring even truer almost two centuries later: on the West Bank the past engulfs all the landscapes, glistens from every hilltop, sidles into every sentence, navigates its way into every contemplation and constantly paints pictures in your mind (including some you do not understand at all).

What drove me to take this journey, however, was not the past but the future. Everyone in Israel is fond of pointing out doubts about its future existence. Cynicism, one-upmanship, biblical clichés and prophesies of doom characterize public discourse—as well as private conversation—about the future, and not by chance. People on both the right and the left in Israel live without a clear picture of their country's future, or even a hazy one. A future apocalypse is ever-present in the back of the mind and sometimes gleaming in its forefront. No one seems truly able to imagine the state of things in 2040 or 2060. Most people do not even have an answer to the simplest of questions: Where will our country's borders run and what sort of state will it be?

Israel, after all, never declared what it intended to do with the West Bank (unlike East Jerusalem, which it formally annexed after the 1967 war), and the result is a lack of definitive borders. Israel controls the West Bank through military law and might, but it has never formalized the occupied territories' status. Yet the presence of the Israeli Defense Forces (IDF) and well over half a million settlers makes it impossible to argue that it is *not*, in fact, part of Israel. Where, then, do Israel's borders run? Clearly not along the pre-1967 lines, since the state now reaches much further than that. Does Israel encompass the West Bank and even beyond? Formally, no.

Yet despite this territorial and existential instability, most of my friends, including the most skeptical and pessimistic ones, have become parents in recent years, while continuing to harbor profound doubts about the country's chances of continuing to exist, certainly in its current structure. Still, they go about their daily lives: they buy apartments, start businesses, save money for their five-year-old's college education. There seems to be a peculiar disconnect between most Israelis' gloomy political outlook and their day-to-day conduct. They have somehow convinced themselves that everything will stay just as it is indefinitely. "And the years were more crushed and crammed and rushed than we were," wrote the poet Israel Pincas, "but we acted as though we were immortal, as though there were time for everything."

I was troubled by this chasm between our bleak political future and our everyday routines—as if we lived in the shadow of the future but actually in denial of its existence. Again and again I asked my friends, political allies and adversaries: What will our future look like? What sort of country will be here? How many countries? Which ones? What laws will they have? Why don't we try to imagine the future together, now? I came to understand that we don't really want to talk about Israel's political future, making do instead with generalizations, complaints and vague predictions peppered with black humor. I realized that what has evolved in Israel over the past few years is a collective repression of the future.

I did not leap into the future, of course, during my travels. But, everywhere I went, I asked about it, I sought solutions and ideas, I invited people to present their plans, draw up borders, and grapple with the implications of their vision. And if they had no vision? I urged them to articulate one. I asked about borders, about citizenship, about identity, I asked about 2040 and 2060. I was determined to put the question to both Jews and Arabs living on the West Bank, the question that has troubled me for years, the most urgent question we face: What will our future here look like?

I did not waste time arguing, preaching, or endlessly voicing my horror. Mostly I wanted the people right in front of me to tell me their stories, and at times to prod them to follow the course of what they told me to its logical outcome, to chafe their political dreams up against the sharp stones of reality, and to leave my readers room to equivocate, to formulate their own positions. This journey, for me, was an opportunity to look straight in the eye of this shapeless demon that awaits us around the bend. And while authors often use whispers, memories, fears and dreams to "turn a demon into a story," on this journey I sought to turn the demon into a political model that would be as lucid as possible— or rather into an assortment of models that contend with the past, the present and the future. Because this is the crux of the matter:

any political model in Israel must grapple with past, present and future, something that most of the familiar models do not do. Instead, they omit one or more of these elements, or they recreate the past in order to bolster the positions of those proposing them. Most often, they err by determining that the whole thing began with Israel's occupation of the West Bank in 1967.

* * *

I've been asked whether this journey has left me more pessimistic or more optimistic. The truth is, I cannot say exactly. Perhaps I should feel more sober, and to some extent I do, but not always. After all, I saw many disheartening things, I learned how convoluted and multifarious the apparatus of the occupation is—a labyrinth that one cannot but get lost in—but I also met people who gave me hope and even inspiration, and I heard new ideas. On balance, I believe that the struggle for a political order in which Jews and Arabs can live with equal rights is far from over. If there is one thing the twentieth century has unequivocally taught us, it is that enormous changes that were previously unthinkable can occur, sometimes in the blink of an eye. There is no divine edict for eternal war in this land. I still believe that we have not done enough, that we have not shown sufficient political courage or genuinely examined fresh ideas, and that all this can still be changed. Despite the views I often heard on my journey, I have to believe that the fate of the people living here still depends on them—on us—and that we still have time.

1

They Yelled *Allahu Akbar*
Balata Refugee Camp

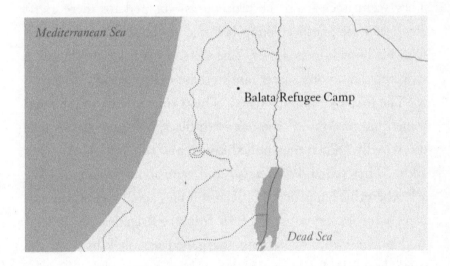

A young boy in an undershirt kneels on a patch of dirt by the side of the road. He is blindfolded with a handkerchief, his back is arched, head bowed, hands tied behind his back. His arms look strong and muscular. The sky above him is a crisp blue, with Mount Gerizim and the Palestinian village of Burin in the background, and sunlit green mountains on the horizon. Young soldiers with cocked rifles surround the boy. None of the passing vehicles stops, and no sound comes from our car. It's a peculiar tableau: the boy, the soldiers, everyone motionless.

The minute we get out of the car, the soldiers rush at us, yelling, "Military zone! Get the hell out of here now!" We ask them repeatedly why the boy is tied up, but they just keep yelling. When our photographer runs past and snaps a few shots of the boy, the soldiers lunge at him, but then they abruptly relent and switch from barking commands to a friendly request that he back off. They seem unclear on the procedures—or perhaps there aren't any. I can see another young boy tied up behind an army jeep with his body hunched over. The sides of his head are shaved, a style popular among soccer fans in these FIFA World Cup days.

The soldiers gradually relax. "They came up to us and shouted something in Arabic," the one with black hair and glasses tells us excitedly. "Then they pulled knives and ran at me!" Another adds, "They yelled *Allahu akbar* and were about to stab us!" We ask when this happened. "Fifteen minutes ago," explain the soldiers, who are serving in the Kfir Infantry Brigade.

I notice two new-looking sharpened assault knives on the jeep's hood, laid out neatly alongside cigarette packs, identity cards, wallets and cell phones.

The soldiers stand the kids up and walk them to another jeep parked on the shoulder. "Where are you taking them?" we ask. A short soldier with a smiling face and a large yarmulke replies, "To the nearest pit. Babi Yar." His friend steps in. "Don't listen to him, he's kidding." The boys are sitting on small benches inside the jeep now. One of the soldiers arranges their legs more comfortably. We ask the kids where they live but they don't answer.

When we speak with a long-time local activist named Zekharia, who works to get Palestinian detainees released, he says stabbing soldiers is a serious offense and he can't help these boys. He's heard they're from Askar, one of a group of refugee camps in the Nablus area that includes Ein Beit al-Ma' and Balata. The black-haired soldier who said he was the first one the boys tried to stab insists: "They came at us with knives and a crazed look in their eyes."

The door slams shut and the jeeps pull away. We drive in the opposite direction, to Balata. Only a few other cars are on the road. We pass heaps of vehicle parts, green tree-lined hills and clusters of single-story houses. The Israeli radio channel Reshet Bet reports: "Near the village of Burin, south of Nablus, soldiers have arrested two Palestinians who approached them and aroused their suspicion. The Palestinians were found in possession of knives." We get to a hilly range populated by wealthy Nablus families and drive past a lavish estate, on the edge of Mount Gerizim, owned by businessman Munib al-Masri. Sprawling across almost seventy-five acres, it is considered the most luxurious estate in Palestine.

The alleyways of Balata Refugee Camp are crowded, the roads dotted with potholes, trash, piles of dirt and sewage. The alleys branch off into long, narrow lanes, just wide enough for one person, and children start to emerge from every lane. Lots of children. "How are you?" they ask in English, over and over again, laughing. The walls are covered with graffiti: a rifle with crosshairs, and not ten yards away two peace doves taking flight. On the main street, the Kasbah, there are clothing shops, produce stands, a small meat restaurant and a few grocery stores. Two little girls in white dresses, one of them holding a queen's scepter, wave hello.

In the United Nations Relief and Works Agency (UNRWA) building, where staff oversee the refugee camp's daily affairs, the offices are abuzz. The building will soon be taken over by doctors from the NGO Physicians for Human Rights, which is holding a temporary clinic here today. The medical care they provide is useful, but the main attraction is the containers full of pharmaceuticals they deliver. More than forty thousand people live in Balata and there is only one medical center here, run by UNRWA, which operates five days a week until 3 p.m. After that time residents can seek medical care elsewhere, in Nablus for instance, but most people here can't afford a private doctor.

The doctors are chatting with directors of the local committee about a topic they are all familiar with: a training course in Tel HaShomer Hospital, near Tel Aviv, to which doctors from Gaza were invited, but which they ultimately decided to boycott under pressure from the BDS (Boycott, Divestment and Sanctions) movement. Participating in the course would have meant collaborating with the Israeli establishment. Some of the Palestinians support the boycott, others object. A young Palestinian nurse told me: "These enticing offers for medical or economic co-operation are part of the normalization of the occupation. The Israelis know we need co-operation to improve our lives, and it's good for their image in Israel and around the world. It happens everywhere, all the time. We face a constant dilemma: collaborate or not."

Now they're discussing the Palestinian minister Ziad Abu Ein, who died in December 2014 after a confrontation with Israeli soldiers. Abu Ein's acquaintances say he used to call them, back when he was being held in Israeli prisons to report on the detainees' conditions. I meet with Ghassan, who chairs a committee set up to resist settler violence in the northern West Bank. He used to work with the late minister. Ghassan says he visits villages that have been attacked by settlers every day, mainly in the Nablus region. "There are twelve settlements around Nablus, with about twenty-five hundred residents, and it's mostly people from Yitzhar settlement who keep attacking the villages. We protect them as best we can."

I tell Ghassan that I recently spoke with West Bank Palestinians who complained about the fecklessness of the Palestinian Authority (PA) in the face of the settlers' "price-tag" operations—burning mosques, smashing windshields, attacking Palestinians, uprooting olive trees. They feel the PA's response isn't forceful enough, that it seems a little fatigued, indifferent even, perhaps wary of confronting the Israeli Defense Forces (IDF). They claim that ad-hoc initiatives like one in the village of Qusra, where a local force has been set up to protect residents from the settlers, are far more efficient. "What kind of talk is that?" Ghassan responds. "We don't have any real power or authority, and the IDF works for the settlers. We document everything, we talk, we take action, we file reports, but complaining to the IDF is useless, and if we respond with violence the army will quickly act against us, which is exactly what the settlers are waiting for. I'm working under impossible circumstances."

We are surrounded by a dozen teenagers wearing orange bandanas and gray vests embroidered with the word "Yafa." They stand quietly listening to the adults. After a while, I sit down outside with them. They don't speak any Hebrew, so their twenty-something-year-old counselor translates. They belong to a youth group, part of the World Organization of the Scout Movement, which has about 150 members in Balata. Their movement has a political consciousness, they explain. "We volunteer and we go on demonstrations," says a boy named Salakh. "The emphasis in our movement is on volunteering. Our goal is to serve the people in the camp. There is a lot of distress in the camp, a lot of unemployment. We help the poor and needy, we clean streets and pathways, and on holidays we have activities and plays." Today they have come to prepare the building for the doctors and help carry containers of medication to the top floor, where an improvised pharmacy has been set up.

"Where are you from?" I ask the boys.

"From Yafa," says one. "Yafa," repeats another. One says Kafr Saaba—the Arab village that lay east of what is now a booming city in Israel's central region and bears the Hebrew name of Kfar Saba. One boy is from Gaza. The vast majority give the names of towns or villages from which their grandparents were displaced in 1948. Salakh tells us that when the Israelis occupied

Kafr Saaba, his family fled to the town of Qalqilya, then to a village near Salfit, assuming they would be able to go home after a few weeks. His grandfather was a farmer who owned lands near Kafr Saaba.

"Have you ever been there?"

"No," they all say. None of them has been to Tel Aviv either.

"What political solution do you believe in?"

"We don't think anything bad about anyone, only good things, and so there will be peace," one boy offers and everyone laughs. "For us, Israelis are the occupation. We all have brothers or cousins who've been killed by your army or are in prison," says a boy with glasses; he puts arms around two of his friends. "We believe in a Palestinian state and living with the Israelis. But you have to understand: there is a difference between an Israeli and a Zionist. Jewish Israelis are people who believe in a certain religion and they have a god. Zionism is a terrorist organization."

Dozens of people are gathered on the second floor of the UNRWA building. They are not waiting for a doctor but for an audience with Ahmad Thouqan, who directs the Department for Refugee Affairs, which is part of the People's Committee in Balata. The Committee is affiliated with the Palestinian Liberation Organisation (PLO)'s Department of Refugees and was founded in 1995, after the PA established its base in the West Bank. There were always similar committees in refugee camps in Jordan and Lebanon, but until the Oslo Accords they were not permitted in the West Bank. Thouqan sits at a large desk in his smoke-filled office, with a group of people who purchased a plot of land near the camp, where they want to build a playground. The main issue is money: there isn't enough. The camp sits on a small area and is extremely crowded. Children have nowhere to play, families have nowhere to stroll.

Thouqan, a chain-smoker in his fifties who is always delivering terse answers over the phone or to his staff, is visibly impatient with his loquacious visitors. Clerks regularly appear on either side of him to show him various documents. Health issues are a major concern for him, he says. The camp is overcrowded, there isn't much sunlight, the air is "not good," and many residents suffer from respiratory disease, high blood pressure and, most prevalently, diabetes. There are some twelve hundred diabetics in the camp, many of them children. The problem is that sometimes they need to be checked several times a day, but the UNRWA clinic closes early and the children have no choice but to see a private doctor. This costs money, as does medication. Residents with jobs might earn fifty to eighty shekels a day (roughly US$13 to $20), and even if a visit to the doctor in Nablus is cheap—roughly twenty shekels, or about US$5—they still can't afford it.

Unemployment is another worry. Thouqan estimates a jobless rate of around thirty-five percent. In recent years many Palestinians who were imprisoned during the Second Intifada have been getting out and coming home to the camp. Most are uneducated and struggle to find work. They want to be part of the PA's security apparatus, but they are usually rejected because they are too old or there aren't any positions or they're simply not wanted. When a man walks out of prison at age thirty-five with no family, no job and no education, the camp must help him, in recognition of his contribution to the Palestinian struggle. "Relatively speaking," Thouqan adds proudly, "we have a lot more prisoners and casualties than they do in Nablus."

Some three hundred residents of Balata were killed in the Second Intifada. Recently, however, confrontations with Israel and the IDF's raids are not the only cause of unrest in the camp. One of the women waiting in line to see a doctor explains: "It's tense here, there are loud noises at night, sometimes gunfire." The PA suspects that some of the armed men in the camp, supposedly members of Fatah, are in fact working for Mohammed Dahlan, their financial backer. Dahlan, who was a senior Fatah figure and head of the Preventive Security Force in Gaza, was expelled from the PA's jurisdiction by President Mahmoud Abbas (Abu Mazen) after the latter suspected Dahlan of attempting to remove him from office. Dahlan now spends a fortune in the West Bank and Gaza in an effort to unseat Abbas. In February there were reports of bloody confrontations in the northern West Bank, particularly in Balata, between PA security forces and Dahlan loyalists, after loyalists opened fire while the PA was carrying out arrests.

I ask Thouqan where he gets resources for running the camp. After all, it can't be from taxes.

"We have a good relationship with the PA," he replies, "mainly with the Prime Minister and with Abu Mazen, who help us. We also get a lot of donations, and there's UNRWA and the PLO, of course. But I'll give you an example of something that's been preoccupying me lately, and can be really frustrating. We have more than five hundred students at universities like An-Najah and Birzeit. Pay here is around twenty-five hundred shekels [US$650] a month. If a family has two kids at college, that means each kid needs about ten thousand shekels [US$2,600] a year for tuition. How can they manage that? Now, the only way for people here to get out of their predicament is to study. Because these are people who don't own land or property, and anyway, there's no commerce here. So this is the reasoning: you study and then move to Ramallah or Saudi Arabia or Dubai, you work there and support your family in the camp until your little siblings grow up, then they go to university and support the family. And then you're free to support your new family."

He shows me a document displaying the number 28,000 with a series of columns next to it. They had requested aid to enable families to send their kids to university, and the PLO had sent 28,000 shekels, which is enough to give small subsidies to fifteen students. Thouqan has roughly two hundred requests, and he spent weeks trying to decide how to distribute the funds. He knows that a university degree allows a graduate to support an entire family for several years. He decided to give the money only to students who have more than three siblings, none of whom is currently at university. This narrowed it down only slightly, as the average family has six children.

Beyond the daily troubles, the question of refugees is at the root of political consciousness in the camp. Everywhere in Balata one can see old maps of pre–1948 Palestine, paintings and pencil drawings, pictures of houses and vistas that signify the world that existed before the Nakba, the Arabic term for the catastrophe of expulsion. When you ask people where they are from, they will often mention the family house from before 1948. Thouqan's own story is a good example.

His family lived in Yafa—he means the Yafa District, he emphasizes, which until '48 was a thriving center of Arab life in Palestine, with some 120,000 residents. His village was called al-Sawalima, and the family owned about twelve acres of land and a large modern house they'd built in the 1940s. They grew oranges, watermelons and other fruit. They had up-to-date equipment, including an engine that pumped water. They were deported in the 1948 war, and roamed for a while, eventually settling in the Balata Refugee Camp in the early fifties. Thouqan's father struggled to recover, constantly comparing his existence in the camp with his previous life. A man with lands, money and social status, whose name was known throughout Yafa, now found himself competing for the same low-paying jobs with a laborer he had brought from Egypt to work his fields. "A mixture of humiliation, anger and shame," says Thouqan.

One day a friend found Thouqan's father a job as a guard. When he was driven to his new workplace the next morning, he was shocked to find himself standing on his very own land. Everything was destroyed except the water pump. "This is my land," he told his new employers. He showed them the pump, pointed to trees he had planted himself. He was in such emotional distress that he had to be hospitalized. Ever since that day, he never wanted to set eyes on the place again. He died in 1990. Thouqan's mother had grown up in the village of Jayyous. After the 1967 war, the land around Jayyous became part of the West Bank, and she received almost two acres from her father. The hopes the family pinned on this inheritance were dashed when, in the early 2000s, Israel built the separation wall, which hit the village of Jayyous especially hard. Sixty percent of its agricultural lands are within the seam zone (the limbo area located between the Green Line and the separation wall), which means Israel controls access to those lands by means of a "permit regime." Residents frequently discover that they are not permitted access to their lands. Since the construction of the wall, the villagers' agricultural output has declined by half to roughly four thousand tons of olives a year. Thouqan says his family's plot isn't worth much anymore. Now he can't even visit it.

I ask him about the two-state vision advocated by his organization, Fatah, and about Abu Mazen's negotiations, which do not address the Palestinian right of return to their land and property.

"There are Palestinians who live in Israel, inside the Green Line, right?" he asks. "So why shouldn't Palestinians who used to live there and were deported not go back to their homes? I'm certainly willing to be a citizen of Israel and even serve in the army."

"So is there no resolution without the right of return for the refugees? You must see," I point out, "that you are asking to completely alter the State of Israel."

"Our lands, our home—that is not something I can give up.

I don't even have the right to. My home is Arab al'Awsat. This is not my home here."

"You've lived here in Balata your whole life."

"Yes, but it's not my home, and it's not the home of anyone who lives here. This is where many people live who were kicked out of their homes and their lands, and those of their parents and grandparents. No one has the right to give those up."

In Chile, home to one of the world's largest Palestinian communities, I heard similar talk recently, when I took part in an event with the Palestinian-Chilean writer Diamela Eltit. After the talk, a young woman whose parents lived in Balata but who was born in Chile came up to me. "There's something you people don't understand," she said. "You talked about time—1967 or 1948—but you didn't talk about space. Our spatial perception is different. For Israelis, Palestinians are in Gaza and the West Bank, but our spatial perception also includes refugee camps in Jordan and Lebanon, and large Palestinian communities around the world. It's a non-linear, truncated space, but it is the space of Palestinian consciousness."

A while ago I read *The Meaning of the Nakba*, a formative account by the Arab intellectual Constantine Zurayk, written in 1948, right after the Nakba. Zurayk writes:

> In my opinion, it is our right and our obligation to recognize the enemy's vast power and to thereby not impose excessive guilt on ourselves. But at the same time, it is our right and obligation to recognize our mistakes and the sources of our

weakness…Worst of all would be to evade this responsibility and shut our eyes to our limitations, and to point the finger at an external factor without seeing our own weakness, flaws, corruption and deficiencies.[1]

Before I part with Thouqan, I ask him one more question. "Do you think that self-reckoning has taken place?"

"I'm not entirely sure," he replies candidly. "There was a reckoning about the Nakba, our failures, our fears, our lack of organization. But sometimes I wonder if we made the changes that were necessary after the Nakba, if we weren't too rigid, whether we wouldn't have become much stronger if we'd had the courage to dig into our wounds with our bare hands."

***

At midday, the Kasbah in Balata is bustling. Ahead of me, a small family—a handsome young mother and father with two children dressed in white—takes a leisurely stroll while sewage flows in the gutters beside them. I sit down for a conversation with Dr Fathi Darwish, a short older man who has had an interesting career in the PLO. He asks if I speak Arabic. I stammer and say I took two courses, and manage to string together a couple of sentences. He laughs. I assume he speaks Hebrew, but like

1   Translated into English from Yehouda Shenhav-Shaharabani's Hebrew translation.

many others he chooses to talk to me in English. In the 1970s he spent time in refugee camps in Lebanon, Syria and Jordan, working on healthcare policies. In the eighties he moved to Tunis and worked in Yasser Arafat's office, and in 1994, after a thirty-year exile, he returned to Palestine with Arafat. He recalls how the Palestinians lined the streets for days to welcome their leader: "We were full of optimism then, for us it was the end of exile. There was hope for the end of the occupation, that our children would have a better future. It was clear to all of us that the end of the occupation was very near."

Darwish was born in 1944 in the Haifa neighborhood of Wadi Nisnas. His family lived on Kings Road (today named Independence Road), on the first floor of a building that had a bakery in the basement. He remembers how, one day during the war in 1948, the smell of bread baking gave way to burning: the bakery was on fire, and his father carried him and his sister outside, where they stood watching the building burn. They moved to the village of Ya'bad, west of Jenin, and then wandered on to other places. There are eleven children in Darwish's family, four born in Haifa and the rest on the West Bank and in Kuwait. "We're a classic example of the dismantled post–1948 Palestinian family. Like a grenade that explodes and the shrapnel flies everywhere, my siblings are scattered around the world. I have brothers and sisters in Kuwait, in Saudi Arabia, in Serbia, in America, in Jordan. I haven't seen some of them for more than twenty-five years."

Darwish is a veteran PLO man. When he talks about the

future, he gives the official PA line: "I believe the government of Israel must reinstate its agreements with the Palestinians and go back to the two-state vision. That means a Palestinian state within the 1967 borders with Jerusalem as its capital, and perhaps minor exchanges of territories. Meanwhile, the settlements are threatening to put an end to it all."

"Are you a two-state advocate?" I ask.

"I don't care if there are two states or one state, the important thing for the Palestinians is that the occupation end and they be given the same rights as Jews."

"It seems fair to say that Abu Mazen gave up on the right of return during negotiations. Do you accept that?"

"All over the world, refugees have the right to return. The refugees—they are a fundamental question in any resolution."

"And the answer?"

"How can I explain to refugees in Syria and Lebanon that a Jew from anywhere in the world can go back to Israel because two thousand years ago he had roots here, but they can't go back to their homes? Most of the Palestinians who were born here and then exiled have homes and land—don't they have the right to come back?"

"So the future you see is two states and the return of refugees to their homes in Israel? Because that is very different from the plan that was under discussion: it's not exactly the familiar two-state solution, but more like one state."

"Ask the kids in Balata where they're from and you'll see they'll tell you: I'm from Acre, I'm from Haifa. All those people must be given an answer. I believe that, if there is goodwill and serious negotiation between the Israelis and the Palestinians, we can reach a solution on the refugee issue."

Darwish's arguments raise an interesting point. Two distinct groups are emerging among Israelis, Palestinians and the international community, with divergent views of the past and conclusions for the future. The factions in each group do not share a common purpose but rather a similar historical perspective. The first group might be labeled "the '67 group," and it includes Israel's center-left and some of its right-wing blocs, the international community, and parts of Fatah. For them, the defining event was the 1967 war and, accordingly, they work toward a two-state solution. This group also includes, of course, Palestinians who do not believe that the 1967 war was the defining event but who nonetheless recognize that it is the international parameter for solving the conflict.

The second and more complex group comprises most of the Israeli right wing, primarily the settlers, as well as Israel's far left, and large parts of Palestinian society; these constituents believe that the defining event was 1948 and the expulsion of the Palestinians from their lands. This is also the root of the settlers' claim that Ramat Aviv (a generally left-leaning Tel Aviv suburb built on the ruins of the Palestinian village Sheikh Munis) is one and the same as Ofra or any other West Bank settlement. Members of this group do not believe that the conflict can be truly resolved, although they may support ideas such as the annexation of parts of the West Bank, a single state, the Palestinians' return as part of a two-state agreement, or, like some Palestinians I spoke with, a notion along the lines of "peace, freedom of movement and equal rights within the framework of an agreement." To them, the key to the solution is contending with 1948. Furthermore, most of the PA representatives who speak of 1967 and the international parameters would agree with Fathi Darwish about the return of the refugees, namely, that "they have the right to return." There are those in this camp who do voice reservations, sometimes extremely significant ones (such as an intent not to "change the character of Israel"), but they will not concede on the principle of return, and so the debate with them is a pendulum that swings between '67 and '48. One thing is clear: most Israelis, including those in the peace camp, are unwilling to acknowledge the Palestinian view of 1948.

Darwish says that if Israelis were to read Palestinian writers and poets such as Ghassan Kanafani, Emile Habibi and Muhammad Ali Taa, who wrote about the expulsion, they would gain an understanding of the Palestinian soul, of the moment when a person loses his home and instantly becomes dispossessed. Taa, for example, describes the expulsion of the residents of Mi'ar (which sat just over ten miles east of Acre), including his family, in the '48 war:

> The people left the village taking few possessions: a blanket or two, pillows, some flour, jugs of olive oil, a pot and a few dishes. My father hoisted a blanket and mattress on his shoulders and carried my brother Mahmoud in his arms. My

mother perched a half-full sack of flour on her head, and held my little sister Alia and a jug of olive oil. I hurried behind her...The men began loading things onto donkeys and mules. The families who had beasts of burden were the fortunate ones. The Jews were entering the village. Sounds of gunshot echoed everywhere. The mosque's dome blew off into the sky. There was a loud thundering. Stones flew in the air and there were thick clouds of smoke. And people set off on their way.[2]

Darwish has been fighting against the Israeli occupation for fifty years, yet he is still optimistic. He has long worked co-operatively with Israel and is now troubled, not to say insulted, by Israel's indifference to the Palestinian issue. "After all the killing, the land grabs, the imprisonments, the checkpoints, we keep explaining to our people that we can live in peace with the Israelis. But they don't believe us anymore. We see the elections in Israel, with not a word about the occupation, about the Palestinians, about our rights. Your elections might as well be taking place in Europe. The Palestinians are constantly engaged with Israelis because we have no choice, the Israelis interfere with every aspect of our lives. But we just seem to bore you now, don't we?" After a pause, he adds, "I was in Tunis on the day Arafat and Rabin signed the accord. But the extreme right murdered Rabin. And in fact they destroyed everything."

---

2 Muhammad Ali Taa, *Time of Lost Childhood*, translated into English from Yehouda Shenhav-Shaharabani's Hebrew translation.

I ask whether he thinks the impending—to his mind—Palestinian state will result from negotiations or only through the strategy of The Hague and BDS.

"We have to use any tool that might end the occupation. We must remember the lessons learned from South Africa: the boycott was a critical tool in that struggle. We're not about to spend another twenty years in negotiations so that a hundred more settlements can be built in the meantime. It appears that going to the UN, the international treaties, BDS, those are the only things that affect the Israelis, who are obsessed with their standing in every other place in the world but don't care what their neighbors think of them. If we don't kick up a fuss around the world and there's no terrorism—we might as well be air for the Israelis."

* * *

On Al-Quds Street between Nablus and Balata, there is heavy traffic. A Palestinian policeman in uniform stands on the side of the road. Two teenaged boys sit in the back seat of his car. One of them looks straight ahead with a stern expression, while the other smiles and lights a cigarette from a red pack of Marlboro. A few hours ago, when they were blindfolded, they probably did not see me but might have heard my voice. They wear jeans and T-shirts. The policeman was recently summoned to the checkpoint, where the Israelis handed him the two boys who earlier that day had been suspected of attempting to stab soldiers. It seems improbable that Israel would simply set free two assault suspects, so why were they let go?

I ask the boys themselves, but they have been instructed by the policeman not to talk, so they just wave and smile. I ask the officer; he doesn't know. Zekharia says that, judging by the findings, the kids were not planning to stab anyone; if they really had attacked the soldiers with knives, there is no chance they'd be sitting here now. The soldiers probably exaggerated or misunderstood or perhaps even fabricated. But we saw the knives, I remind him. He asks the Palestinian officer about the knives. No answer. He asks the boys again; they say nothing.

Lots of organizations and people here—the IDF, human rights organizations, the settlers, the PA, various officials—spread rumors and conflicting accounts of every event, particularly those that get little attention in the media. Every story has a competing—or contradictory—version and, in the absence of one fact-checking authority that is acceptable to everyone, each side clings to its own version. These sorts of incidents happen frequently, and in a few days no one will remember these two kids anyway. I ask if they're going home now, to Askar. The answer, as I understand it, is affirmative albeit evasive. I repeat my question but the second answer is even more oblique. The Palestinian policeman says goodbye and drives away. It's drizzling, and the wind is getting cold. It'll be evening soon. Zekharia is talking to someone on the phone about some olive trees that the settlers cut down, and a house on the edge of the village that was stoned.

* * *

It's been two months since my visit to Balata. In a little café in Hawara—a serene village south of Nablus full of auto shops, restaurants and confectionaries—I meet attorney Zidan. A young man of twenty-five, he wears a black sweater-vest and a tight-fitting blazer, with a fashionable goatee and sideburns. His voice is gentle and he has a shy, winning smile. We speak in English. He studied law in Jordan and started a small practice in Nablus two years ago, which takes different types of cases. This week he is in court in Nablus defending a Palestinian charged with selling hashish: a trifling affair, since he only sold to his friends.

At the end of 2014, Zidan was contacted by the parents of one of the two boys from Askar—the younger was seventeen and the other just eighteen—who asked him to represent them against the PA. As it turns out, the car they were in that Saturday did not take them back to Askar but to the PA's prison in Nablus. They were charged with illegal possession of a weapon. Zidan was denied a request to visit his new clients. When I describe for him the scene I saw near Burin a few minutes after they had allegedly tried to stab the soldiers, he smiles dismissively. "They got to the checkpoint and said to the soldiers, 'We have knives, we want you to arrest us.'"

I tell him the soldiers claimed they'd yelled *Allahu akbar*.

Now he laughs. "Maybe they did also yell *Allahu akbar*."

"Why did they want to get arrested?"

"All sorts of reasons," Zidan explains. "Sometimes Palestinians turn up at a checkpoint with knives without any intention of stabbing soldiers. They want to be arrested so that their families will get money, or to earn a matriculation certificate, or because someone in their family is being accused of collaborating with Israel."

"But I'm talking about these particular boys," I insist. "Do you know why your clients did it?"

"They're poor, they had no jobs, no nothing, they wanted to be arrested to get money from the PA. The PA gives money to prisoners in Israeli prisons. That's the whole story, it happens all the time."

I tell him I heard they were in prison for thirty-six days. How did they get out?

"I filed a petition to drop the charges because they didn't have any weapon or anything really dangerous, just knives," he answers, "but the petition was denied. I filed another one and it was denied. I persisted and kept filing petitions to drop the charges. On the fourth petition they suddenly notified me that the investigation was over and there was no evidence against my clients and they let them go. I didn't understand the whole procedure, it was the first time I'd worked on a case like this. When they got out of prison I met them for the first time."

Zidan says the boys were only in prison for twenty-two days; later he claims it was just over two weeks. I ask if the PA kept the kids in prison to scare them, and he gives a circuitous response. Zidan is wary of criticizing the PA, the courts or the police. He is demonstratively courteous but gives brief answers. According to him, one of the two kids has found a construction job in the

Jenin area, which makes his parents happy, and the other is at home but his father makes sure he doesn't get into trouble. Zidan prefers that we not photograph him. He's in a hurry to get back to Nablus. Competition among lawyers is stiff, he says, everyone wants cases, doesn't matter what kind—criminal, civilian, commercial, big, small—as long as you get clients. Fortunately, he's very busy these days.

2

Yes, We're in a Post-Two-State Era

El Matan Outpost and Ma'ale Shomron Settlement

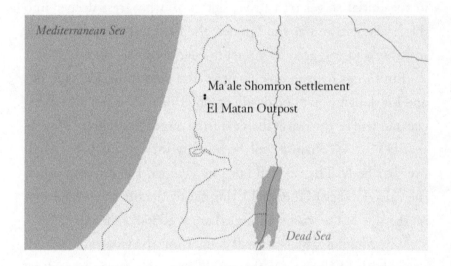

The road from Ma'ale Shomron, an upper-middle-class settlement populated by both religious and secular families, to the outpost of El Matan is narrow and tortuous. We drive up a steep, potholed incline with the houses of Ginot Shomron, the largest neighborhood in yet another settlement, Karnei Shomron, on our right. As the crow flies, the distance between the two communities is small but, since some of the lands in the area are privately owned by Palestinians, the road takes a long and meandering route. It is quiet here, and as the road winds on we see virtually no people, cars or houses, only hills and green valleys and the rocky ridges around us. The sunlight glimmers on the high rocks and suddenly seems to dive down and blind us. As always in the West Bank, these bucolic views, which tend to remind me of the south of France, can be deceptive. The silence might give way to a clamor at any moment. You are often unaware of the discrepancy in the initial stages of a drive, but as you progress deeper into the landscape, and as time passes, the facts fall away from your memory and you gradually start to believe this scenery.

But things happen quickly here. Ten days from now, a father and his daughter will be driving along this road when a Molotov cocktail will be thrown at their car from one of the hilltops. Eleven-year-old Ayelet Shapira will be severely injured, with burns all over her body. The car will burn to a cinder. I have yet to watch the video footage of the smoldering car to identify the precise spot on the side of the road we traveled on. It all looks the same.

The Molotov assailants will come from the village of Azzun, near Ma'ale Shomron. On this sort of road, where one must drive slowly and is often forced to an almost complete standstill because of the twists and turns, it's easy to ambush vehicles from a hill-top. The old road to Ma'ale Shomron went through the center of Azzun, creating daily friction between the settlers and the Palestinians. But as my driver, Dani Dayan, a candidate in the primaries for the religious right-wing party Ha'Bayit Ha'Yehudi ("The Jewish Home") and the former director of the Judea and

Samaria Council (known everywhere by its Hebrew acronym the Yesha Council), says, "Once, in order to get home, I used to go through the middle of Azzun or even Qalqilya. Then the bypass road around Qalqilya was built, and they paved a road past Azzun, too. In terms of the bypass roads, the Oslo Accords did us an excellent service: we no longer had to drive through Palestinian towns, suddenly it was more convenient and pleasant to get to the settlements, and that gave a very big push to the settlement endeavor." But, as it turns out, although the ring roads mean you no longer see the Palestinians from Azzun—they're still here.

The villagers of Azzun, which has a population of about ten thousand and is located in Area B (meaning it is under Palestinian civil control and Israeli security control), have different concerns about the roads. The eastern access to Azzun, which runs alongside Ma'ale Shomron and Karnei Shomron, was blocked in 1990. The army sometimes blocks the main entrance, too, which leads to Highway 55, and then residents must take a side road about a mile and a half long that connects Azzun with the village of Izbat al-Tabib. When the army blocks that road, all that's left is an even more circuitous route.

As we drive, Dayan recounts how the outpost was established in 1992.

"What does 'legal' mean?" he repeats my question curiously. "It means the government says: You build it, and everything will be okay. The outpost wasn't built on Palestinian lands. There was a Supreme Court case about the synagogue located there and in the end they sealed it off. At some point there were five families living there, and, as Jews do, they split into two camps. So my wife and I used to mediate between them. On Sabbaths the place was empty, and we would do guard duty so that someone would be there."

"I've been to see the main settlement," I tell Dayan. "It looks expansive and the houses are set far apart. You don't lack for space. Why was it so important for you to set up the outpost?"

"Because if we hadn't, the lands wouldn't have ended up in Jewish hands," he proclaims. "Someone would have taken them over, and we'd see shepherds and then a tent and in the end there'd be an Arab presence there. It's a zero-sum game: land that isn't theirs is ours, and land that isn't ours is theirs." Dayan recalls stark disagreements about the outpost among Ma'ale Shomron residents. The founding core of the settlement was composed of psychotherapists and social workers—a spoiled upper middle class with no interest in grand adventures, he observes. Some of them didn't want to set up the outpost because it was an illegal move. "In the end I burst out at the secretariat's meeting and yelled at them that that was exactly why we came here."

It is true that El Matan was built on Israeli state-owned lands, but it did not obtain permits from the Ministry of Defense or the government. Nevertheless, government entities, including the Ministry of Construction and Housing, invested funds in the outpost's infrastructure. Although Dayan insists the outpost was founded in 1992, other sources (including activist groups' reports and press coverage) state that it was founded in or around 2000.

In 2010 the Supreme Court ruled that El Matan's synagogue structure must be sealed off, after it was found to encroach on the Qanah River nature reserve. In 2012 it was reported that the government was planning to approve the outpost and recognize it as an artists' village. Gershon Mesika, head of the Shomron Regional Council, claimed at the time: "This is a specific designatory change from an area of tourism structures to one with tourism structures adjacent to a few residential structures... It is a plan that was authorized by me as early as 1999, under Barak's government, and its final signing was dragged out for political reasons." Hearings are currently underway at the Civil Administration to consider objections filed by local Palestinians. Among other things, they oppose the appropriation of almost twenty-five acres of the nature reserve in favor of "agricultural land." Dani Dayan is not bothered by these matters and says final approval is a matter of time.

***

A weary soldier wearing a bulletproof vest patrols a water tower and a bus stop. Around the bend, a row of fairly old white mobile homes lines the shoulder of the road. Cars are parked next to the mobile homes and two children run around outside, too close to the edge of the gorge. No one else is in sight and we hear no voices. I ask Dayan how people can move around here at night when the gorge is so close and so deep. "There are harder things," he says, dismissing my concern. At the front of the outpost is an impressive house with brown roof tiles and window-boxes with flowers. The landscape around us is wild and rocky and there are almost no other houses, not even on the distant horizon. Next to the water tower we meet a young couple here for a visit; they are considering moving to the outpost. The man is secular, and his last name is Sharabi—a common name for Jews of Yemenite origin—while his religious wife, who grew up on the West Bank settlement of Yitzhar and whose last name is Manzowski, is clearly Ashkenazi. Dayan immediately asks her about another Manzowski he knows. The couple was recently married and she is studying at Tel-Hai College, in Israel's far north. They live in Kiryat Shmona, but her studies are almost finished and they want to leave the north and move to the Shomron. They're looking at places like Har Hemed, a newer neighborhood in the established settlement of Kedumim, or perhaps an apartment in the settlement of Tzufim. "The mobile homes are too crowded here," they complain, "and they're made of plaster. Every time someone coughs in one, you hear it in the others. There's no privacy."

I ask if they can picture themselves living here. It's quiet and the views are impressive, but at certain times it would be easy to imagine the quiet becoming an oppressive silence. Besides, the only way out is on that winding road.

"This is a place for pioneers," they decide. "We're not pioneers. We're not looking for this sort of place, but for a mixed religious–secular population, a community settlement, somewhere affordable. We want to pay fifteen hundred shekels (about US$400) a month." They are not particularly impressed by the atmosphere in El Matan, and even less so by the available housing. "We're not worried about the legality of the outpost, that's not part of our consideration, those things always work out."

Both these visitors were born roughly when the outpost was built, in the early 1990s, and the settlements and outposts are, to them, an incontrovertible fact. Their interest in moving to an outpost is not politically motivated—as far as they are concerned, the battle has already been won. They talk very little about politics, saying only that it's easier to set up outposts here than on the mountain ridge. "On the ridge you set up an outpost and next thing you know they shut you down." I tell them that, according to the new plans, the mobile homes will be removed and replaced by an artists' village with forty residential units. They can't wait that long.

"Look." Dani Dayan points to the trailers. "People have been living here for twenty years. In winter, in snow, in the cold, with no electricity. That's why we're winning."

I point out that this young couple seems more concerned about material matters.

"We'll always have enough people to carry out the mission," he replies. "Don't worry about that."

Ma'ale Shomron is an attractive community of about one thousand residents, and it looks slightly different from other settlements I've seen. Narrower, tree-lined streets, handsome villas with distinct designs, set further apart from one another. In the well-manicured yard at Dayan's single-family house, I meet a tall, broad-shouldered, muscular man with red hair. He is currently working as a gardener for Dayan, but I quickly learn about his glory days: this is the man who founded El Matan. He habitually avoids anyone he perceives as a "left-wing writer," but finds it hard to resist an invitation to retell the tale of the outpost's origins. Given the conflicting information about El Matan's birth date, I ask this new source for his version.

It all started one summer day in the mid-1990s, he recalls. He and his wife were at her parents' home in the next settlement over, Karnei Shomron, and he told her he felt like doing something. She said if he really meant it and wasn't just grandstanding, then she wanted a settlement, right there—she pointed out the window to an area some distance away. He decided to make her wish come true. There was nothing there, just earth, not even a road. They pitched a tent and lived in almost complete isolation. After a while, he checked the maps to find out exactly where there was Arab-owned land, where the nature reserve was, and where there was non-privately owned land. One evening he called Zeev Hever, a long-time leader of the settler movement with strong ties to politicians, who told him if he really wanted to set up a new community, they should meet as soon as possible.

The man with red hair arrived for the meeting with a map and pointed to a few possible locations. They picked one. Hever asked how many households were involved in the plan, and the redhead said about sixty. In truth, he didn't even have five families. A bigger meeting was arranged, in Jerusalem, and he was told to come with the other families' representatives. So he rounded up a few friends and persuaded them to skip work for a day. On the way he told one of them to say he was in charge of security, another that he oversaw water and supplies, and so forth. They got to the meeting and made a good impression, and the next day they were summoned to another meeting in Jerusalem. The five friends wouldn't give up another day of work, so the founder recruited some new ones. At the end of that meeting, Hever said: "Do you think we're idiots? You show up to each meeting with different people." The man with red hair explained that there was a core group of sixty families who all wanted to be at the meetings, so he invited different ones each time.

After a while, the settlement movement's main organization, Amana, paved a narrow road to the outpost at a cost of half a million US dollars, donated a few mobile homes and sent over some security guards. "We got about fifty acres," my interlocutor brags, "and if we hadn't done that, the Arabs would have taken over the land. I even raised sheep. I had a hundred and fifty head, so we could take over as much land as possible."

An interesting story, I observe. Romantic, even. When this man set up the outpost, he was the same age as the couple we met in El Matan who said the plaster walls were too thin.

The large living room in Dani Dayan's spacious home opens up into the kitchen. There is a big library upstairs, and a reading nook with a view of the mountains. On the walls are drawings, sculptures and masks from all over the world, including several post-colonial artifacts from Africa and elsewhere, and a singing bowl for meditation. Dayan refused to visit South Africa as long as it was under apartheid rule and went for the first time when

Nelson Mandela became president. He says Israel's relations with the apartheid regime are a blemish on its record. Dayan and his wife are secular and came to Ma'ale Shomron after the 1988 elections, at the height of the First Intifada, joining about forty other families, both religious and secular. They had previously lived in Tel Aviv, although even Israel's biggest city was a recreational wasteland as far as Dayan was concerned: he immigrated to Israel in 1971 from Buenos Aires, a city that only really starts moving at midnight. But he absorbed the pervasive sense of being part of a common cause, which David Ben-Gurion had successfully instilled in Israelis. He says that when Tel Aviv's legendary mayor, Shlomo "Chich" Lahat, "brought about the huge positive revolution and turned a small sleepy town into a massive metropolis, he also drained the city, and secular Israel, of its Jewish roots and its sense that there was a mission to carry out here; what was left was a sort of hedonism."

Dayan is always on the phone. This is our second meeting and there have been some changes in his life since the first. Although he is close to Prime Minister Benjamin Netanyahu, last week he declared his candidacy in the primaries for Ha'Bayit Ha'Yehudi, openly encouraged by the party's leader, Naftali Bennett. With two months to go before the election, the party is climbing steadily in the polls, Bennett's campaign is a hit, and there is talk of sixteen seats (out of 120 in the Knesset, the Israeli parliament) and even of surpassing Netanyahu's leading Likud Party. At least for now, Ha'Bayit Ha'Yehudi's future looks brighter than ever. Dayan claims he doesn't really want to be in the Knesset but accepted the party's call: he was told his voice as a secular settler with intimate knowledge of the international community could be an asset. His distaste for "careerism" is reminiscent of the 1960s Labor Party stalwarts, which for him would be a flattering comparison. He doesn't yet have a campaign headquarters or activists, and he faces widespread opposition because he is completely secular. He is debating how to answer questions about his position on same-sex marriage. If he tells the truth—that he supports it—his election prospects will plummet.

"Would it be akin to a Republican candidate in the US being pro-abortion?" I ask.

Dayan does not look amused.

Apart from same-sex marriage, there is another reason why Dayan's positions put him closer to today's Likud than to Ha'Bayit Ha'Yehudi: unlike his colleagues, he sees the settlement enterprise as a political tool rather than a purpose in and of itself. Invoking Herut, the staunchly right-wing precursor to the Likud Party, he explains: "Herut never sanctified the settlements or sought a Messiah here. It saw the settlements as a political act. I believe that an Israel that willingly gives up Hebron and Beit El would become a hollow society."

"There are those who view Israeli society as hollow even with the settlements," I remark. "What, in fact, is a society that is not hollow?"

"I'm a maximalist Zionist," he says, not exactly answering my question. "The goal of Zionism is to have the entire Jewish people in the entire Land of Israel. The chain of Jewish existence here is my life's mission. I am absolutely secular, but Zionism is my true religion. In Tel Aviv there is no religion and no Zionism and what's left is a form of hedonism."

"We've heard plenty of talk about hedonistic secularism," I begin to tell him. "That's not why we're here. I'm interested in something I've noticed in my conversations with settlers: among a certain elite in your demographic, and perhaps also among younger people, there is a sense of moral erosion. It's becoming increasingly difficult to justify your supremacy over the Palestinians in every realm of life, and their status as a people without rights and without citizenship. This coin has two sides: firstly, the status quo is untenable in the pragmatic sense, because of the implications for Israel's status and future if it continues to deny the Palestinians their rights—you know this because you are exposed to the voices coming from the rest of the world. But there is also the question of morality. While the settlers frequently invoke a moral argument to make their case, you cannot really justify the Palestinians' status in the West Bank, morally speaking. One solution to this predicament, perhaps the more decent one, was proposed by Uri Elitzur [an influential journalist and publicist from Israel's religious right wing], who said that, if we want the Land of Israel, we must pay the price by offering all Palestinians citizenship in a single state. Others, including yourself, equivocate among all sorts of plans meant to bring about incremental change in the situation. But there are also those settlers who understand that we must—even if only apparently—come to grips with the issue of the Palestinians' lack of rights and status."

YES, WE'RE IN A POST-TWO-STATE ERA   47

Dayan accepts this premise. "There are two real narratives here," he explains, "and even King Solomon would not be able to pronounce which is correct. We say this is our land, we were banished from it and have always longed to return. And one day a giant statesman, namely Theodor Herzl, turned that longing into a national emancipation movement. The Palestinians say King David might have lived around here or he might not have. It's folklore or fiction, and anyway it's irrelevant. They see us as a classic European nineteenth-century colonial power. There is no compromise between these two narratives. It will end only when one side gives up its aspirations. But there are wrongs that can be righted even without a solution to the bigger issue. I'm talking about human rights, freedom of movement for the Palestinians, unnecessary roadblocks, rehabilitating the refugee camps, obstacles we put in their way to prosperity."

"Why are you bothered by all that?"

"I went on a tour of the checkpoints led by Machsom Watch," he said, referring to the group of Israeli women who monitor the conduct of soldiers and police at checkpoints in the West Bank, "and things don't look good. There is a moral problem here and it is also a political need of Israel's. Here, unlike with land, there is no zero-sum game. I gain nothing from Palestinian suffering. If we want to stay in Judea and Samaria, the Palestinians must be able to live normal lives. It can't be that people in the twenty-first century can't conduct normal lives. It can't go on forever. When a Palestinian stands waiting at a checkpoint while a soldier texts his girlfriend—there is no justification for that."

Dayan has spent a lot of time in Washington, DC, and in European Union circles, and name-drops people like Milton Friedman and Condoleezza Rice. He also meets with ambassadors and journalists from all over the world, and notes that this very living room was described in a *New York Times* profile. He is something akin to a foreign minister for the settlers. The way he sees it, his status stems from the evolving relationship (which in the past did not exist) between the settlers and the rest of the world: the settlers have an interest in the international community's position and perhaps in altering or at least softening it, while the world has an interest in the settlers' position, or at least understands that they are a force not to be ignored. "A few years ago I spoke at the Israeli Presidential Conference and afterwards some ambassador sat down next to me. I asked to meet with him. He didn't get back to me. Now he calls me up every three months to schedule a meeting. There is huge curiosity about our opinions."

He looks too self-satisfied, and I needle him. "It would be hard to argue that you've changed the international community's views on the illegality of the settlements, or that you've managed to wean it off the two-state idea."

"That is true. But at least we have gradually won a seat at the table. When I go to DC, I'm the first settler who gets through the gates to the White House and the State Department. There is also a more cynical explanation of the attitude toward me. Someone in the State Department told me: 'For years we saw you as agents of the Israeli government's policy, but we finally figured out that you are autonomous and that the Israeli government is an agent of your policy.' As far as coming around on the two-state solution, I believe that Obama and Clinton realized that, in the short and medium term, it's a dead horse. There are also European ambassadors who will tell you that, confidentially. But on one issue my efforts have completely failed: changing international opinion about construction in Judea and Samaria. I've gained receptive ears when it comes to policy, but not about construction."

"Could it be that in speaking of easing restrictions on the Palestinians, you're focusing on the wrong piece of reality? Perhaps their lives will never be normal as long as you are around? Because if they have no state and no vote to influence the regime that determines their fate, they are in an inherently abnormal situation."

"I'm not a stickler. I'm willing to commit injustices for the sake of the Jewish people's existence. But you have to understand: for twenty years the whole system has been managed with the assumption that the two-state solution is around the corner, and all matters of daily life were postponed. After John Kerry's failure, it's now clear that the road does not lead to two states. And so we need an initiative. There will not be two states, a single state is a disaster, unilateral withdrawals have led nowhere. And so the only plan is to give significant relief to the Palestinians now. I'm not asking anyone to give up their aspirations, I'm rehabilitating the refugee camps without demanding anything of them. I'm not expecting them to give up the right of return, but I do want their lives to improve."

"Are the two-state proponents being dishonest with them-selves?"

"Yes, we're in a post-two-state era. John Kerry breathed new life into the two-state idea, but ultimately his failure was the proof. I believe we've been in a post-two-state era since 2010. Anyone who genuinely examines Obama's first two years in office, as compared to the following two, will see that he came to realize it was impossible and he dropped the subject. So we must abandon the purely political track and continue on the humani-tarian, human track."

"So you're willing to give the Palestinians everything except their own state or the right to vote in a binational state?"

"That's a fairly accurate definition."

"Let's say we adopt your suggestion now and the Palestinians' condition improves. In your proposal there is no plan for Israel in another forty years. You don't really have any future vision."

"I have very amorphous ideas about the future. I'm not present-ing them now because they'd sound like political science fiction. Especially when we're under the tyranny of the two-state solution."

"You just said we're in the post-two-state era. Let's agree there are no two states—what will Israel look like in four decades?"

"I'll give you the criteria: (a) every person must be a full citi-zen of the state that controls his fate; (b) no one is deported from his home; (c) Israel is a Jewish and democratic state; (d) there is no foreign sovereignty west of the Jordan."

"It seems to me that (a), (c) and (d) contradict each other sev-eral times over."

"Not in the world I'm depicting in a few decades."

"Your criteria are impossible," I protest. "If it's a binational state, you can't assert that it will be forever Jewish and democratic. And you don't want two states. So where exactly will the Palestinians be full citizens—in Brazil? Maybe you're just adroitly dancing around Uri Elitzur's proposal: one state for everyone. Are you unwilling to adopt it because you know it has no chance for support in Jewish society, or do you really object to a single state?"

"There are people among the settlers, mostly intellectuals, who have adopted the one-state idea. They are excited by the notion of imposing sovereignty over all of the Land of Israel. They don't really understand the cost. I'm not there and most of the settlers aren't there. I want a Jewish democratic state."

"Then we'll have to go back to science fiction: what is your plan for the future?"

"If you insist, and I know this will not be acceptable now, I aspire to two sovereign states with the Jordan River as their border. The State of Israel to the west and the State of Jordan, or an Arab-Palestinian state, to the east. But even though the Jordan River is the border, the Arab-Palestinian state will have full authority over the Palestinians in Judea and Samaria. I mean functional sovereignty, not territorial. Does such a thing exist today? No."

"This is," I tell him, "a return to the familiar formula of Jordan as the Palestinian state, with a few moderating elements thrown in. I guess there are no original ideas left, only new permutations of existing ones. Perhaps you understand that the idea doesn't stand a chance, and your position is this: continue the existing circumstances with certain improvements in the Palestinians' lives. Or a sort of throwback to the pre–First Intifada Oslo Accords era, with less separation between Palestinians and Jews and greater freedom of movement?"

"Roger Cohen wrote in the *New York Times* that the status quo is sustainable. Meaning, it can be maintained for the foreseeable future. I also think the existing situation is tolerable. But it has to be improved. Before the First Intifada my Arab neighbor could say to his kids: 'It's a nice day, let's go to Tel Aviv,' and my father used to go to a dentist in Qalqilya. I would like to see engineers from Ramallah working in the high-tech campus of Kiryat Atidim in Tel Aviv. Acknowledge the abnormalities of the situation and create as much normalcy as possible within it. I am critical of Israeli society. We're not interested in the Palestinians' aspirations. Telling them I can't fulfill their aspirations doesn't mean I deny them. When a candidate for President of the United States said there was no Palestinian nation, the settlers cheered. But it's not a historical matter, it is a political aspiration. Those who say today that there is no Palestinian nation are lying to themselves."

"Some commentators think the idea that the international community will step in and make things right is a fiction told by the left wing for decades. Because the truth is that the world continues to arm us and maintain close economic ties with us. Israel is able to uphold an occupation regime and to prosper economically and keep up trade relations with most of the world. Maybe, on this question, the right wing has won and you have proved that we can be an occupier without paying a heavy price in the international arena?"

"I guess, unlike you," he laughs, "I'm a little more concerned about the boycott movement. I can already tell what a psychological effect it's having on the Prime Minister. If we have to drink Turkish coffee instead of espresso, I'm not worried, but I see that lots of other people are. The boycott is still very remote. Maybe there will be sanctions on the settlements, but that won't have much of an effect because the settlement enterprise does not rely on industry but on the number of residents. And that number keeps going up. Remember: all this talk aside, that is the one constant."

3

You're the First
Jew He's Ever Seen
Ramallah

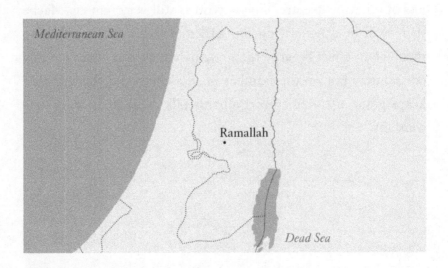

The southern outskirts of Ramallah are visible at the end of the tunnel we're driving through. To my left and right, there is a different sovereignty on either side. "How can this be separated?" asks my companion, who has long ago lost faith in the two-state idea. "Any separation is a contrived act that torments the people who live here. You come into a space they used to move in freely and you put up a wall, and borders, and questions of sovereignty.

That doesn't interest them, they want to move around."

A convoy of cars crawls in front of us, honking constantly. We've reached the Kalandia checkpoint, which more than ten thousand people cross every day. At Ben Gurion Airport, according to a friend who works there, the daily traffic is roughly thirty thousand passengers. Vehicles arrive at Kalandia from every direction, and pedestrians squeeze their way between them. It smells of smoke and charcoal, and a thin boy sleeps on a ripped maroon sofa with a charred armrest. No one looks at us when we drive through. They'll only stop us on the way back.

We pass the houses of Kafr 'Aqab, a neighborhood that was annexed by Israel after the '67 war, then drive past scaffolded buildings of all sizes and styles, sometimes so close to each other that the jumble of concrete above us seems to cohere into a single band. The building shells are punctuated by semitrailers, heaps of dirt, pick-up trucks and cement mixers: a construction boom.

The separation wall towers above us, adorned with colorful murals of Yasser Arafat and the imprisoned Palestinian leader Marwan Barghouti. The road is extremely bumpy. What sovereignty are we under now? I ask. "Israeli," I'm told, "technically, you're still in Jerusalem." Jerusalem? The answer surprises me. Jerusalem is where I grew up, and this octopus with tentacles reaching out in every direction is much larger than the map of the city I hold in my mind.

In Ramallah, Palestinian policemen direct traffic. I think back to a rainy visit three months ago, when this street was a frothy canal of polluted water that threatened to swallow up the cars at any moment. We got lost that time, and ended up on the outskirts of town, where we stepped out of the car and watched the rain beating down on the hills. A few large pine trees with broad tops towered over the blanket of olive trees, which looked like their little children.

The sky is a clear blue now, as we wind our way down a long, narrow street to an inconspicuous building that houses the office of Munir Abushi, who oversees various political initiatives. We sit in a small office with Munir, Awni al-Mashni, Muhammad al-Beiruti and Radi Jarai. They are all in their sixties or older, and all served time in Israeli prisons during the seventies and eighties—eight-, ten-, twelve-year terms. I ask why they were imprisoned. They laugh and give ambiguous answers. Munir says he and al-Beiruti were arrested in the same week in 1974; they were both PLO activists. "I told him: 'Hide, they're coming to arrest you this week,'" he teases al-Beiruti. In those days Munir was a student in Damascus and occasionally used to cross the border into the West Bank to visit family or take part in political activities. He boasts of being "Israel's most wanted man" in the seventies, but his friends claim he's exaggerating.

I ask about their years in Be'er Sheva Prison together. At first it was tough, they say, but then—and their faces suddenly twinkle with laughter—it was good. Only Awni's expression remains blank; he is usually focused on the matter at hand and has no patience for these rituals and gestures, whose necessity he nonetheless recognizes.

Their nostalgic smiles surprise me. "Was it good for every-one?" I ask.

"Yes," they nod. At first the wardens were always interfering in their lives, so they kicked up a fuss and went on strike. There was a full-scale prison riot, and friends of theirs were killed. In the end they "beat the prison," and the wardens stepped back and let them manage their own affairs. They were "a whole gang" in prison, men aged from fifteen to seventy, from every social class, all packed into huge rooms at night. Every morning they got up, had breakfast together, sometimes worked out, held lessons for those who were illiterate, and then read books for perhaps eight or ten hours.

They read everything: world literature classics, fiction, poli-tics, sociology, philosophy—from Frantz Fanon to Theodor Herzl. A guy named Khaled studied *Altneuland* (Herzl's utopian novel outlining his vision for the future Jewish state); he is sup-posed to join us soon. "It was a good time," al-Beiruti reiterates. "I can't remember a period when we had as much autonomy to conduct our own lives as we did in prison. We slept, rested, read, spoke about the future. Apart from women, we had everything." In prison they learned about Jewish society and history, and for-mulated their political principles together. They started getting to know the Israeli side, learned the stories Jews believe in. One thing they still don't understand, or perhaps refuse to accept, is the desire of most Jews to separate from Arabs.

They got out of prison in the late eighties and had to rebuild their lives from scratch. Munir eventually became the governor of

Salfit, a Palestinian town near the huge settlement of Ariel. Most of them held senior positions in the Palestinian security forces and are well acquainted with the subtleties of Palestinian politics. Al-Beiruti wrote a book about Palestinian prisoners, *The Sun Is Born from the Mountain*. "Do you know how many Palestinians have been through the Israeli prison system since 1967?" he asks me. "Men who spent between one day and twenty years in there?"

I confess that I don't know the answer, but I'm a gambler. "One hundred and fifty thousand?"

"Around eight hundred thousand," he whispers.

Munir laughs. "You should have seen your face!"

Many years have gone by since their release. After their PLO activities, the years in prison, the families they started, jobs in the Palestinian Authority, political and business careers for some, they are now involved in an Israeli–Palestinian peace initiative called "Two States One Homeland," the culmination of their political lives and hopes for the future. I've been involved in the initiative from its inception, and this is our fourth meeting. Every time we meet I look at them and wonder how, after all these years, they still have faith.

The atmosphere is tense today. Rather than lounging on their creaking wooden chairs, exchanging quips with us, the Palestinians shift uncomfortably, fire their comments out, and scrutinize the language of the statement of principles we've come up with. There is a reason for their agitation: in about two hours we will drive to the Fatah headquarters in Ramallah to meet Muhammad al-Madani, a member of the Central Committee of

Fatah and the chairman of a PA committee in charge of relations with Israeli society. It is the first time we are presenting our initiative to a senior PA representative.

A bulky man with a loud, hoarse voice arrives late to the meeting. "Here's Khaled, the Herzl expert," someone hisses. Khaled, who lives in Hebron, is accompanied by a little boy wearing a brown leather jacket and a bored look on his face. The boy shakes my hand formally, sits down in a corner and stares at us, and I notice something odd: he's not playing with a smartphone. They live near the Chabad-Lubavitch plot of the ancient Jewish cemetery in Hebron's Tel Rumeida neighborhood. "Not many Palestinians," someone comments, "have stayed on in H2."

The H2 label is less familiar than its A, B and C counterparts. Area A designates lands under full Palestinian control; Area B sections are under Palestinian civil administration but Israeli security control; Area C is under Israeli civil and security control. In 1997, Netanyahu's government signed an agreement with the PA pertaining to Hebron, which at the time was the last remaining Palestinian city with an IDF presence. The agreement divided the city into two areas: H1, which would be under full Palestinian control, and H2, which remained under Israeli control and was populated by some twelve hundred Jewish settlers and roughly forty-five thousand Palestinians.

In the years since the agreement, many Palestinians have abandoned the H2 area, and Khaled's stories make it clear why. Two weeks ago, settlers smashed his living-room windows, and then his fifteen-year-old son was stopped near Shuhada Street by Israeli soldiers, who broke his leg. Last week all the residents of his building, including the children, were pulled out onto the street at 10 p.m. by army orders and left standing there until 2 a.m. "All my son sees is settlers and soldiers," Khaled says. "I dragged him here so he could see that there are other Jews too." He speaks in Hebrew—he also served time in Be'er Sheva—but the boy only speaks Arabic.

Munir then tells an interesting story. In 1996, right after Netanyahu's first election victory, the governor of Jenin got a phone call: "Minister Ariel Sharon wants to see you. You don't have to come. Only if you want to." Sharon met the governor and asked him: If it were on the table, do you think the West Bank Palestinians would be willing to accept Israeli citizenship? In response, the governor asked: Would Gaza residents get citizenship too? Sharon grew irate at the mention of Gaza; he wanted to know about the West Bank. All the men present are familiar with the story. Al-Beiruti claims it was the idea behind Israel's 2005 disengagement: get rid of Gaza, annex the West Bank and offer its residents some type of citizenship.

Khaled observes: "After more than a hundred and twenty years of Zionism, after all their ploys, the Jews are still a minority in the Land of Israel, and they live with constant violence and war. The national Palestinian movement has also failed, since it hasn't been able to get rid of the occupation. If everyone here realizes they've failed, we might be able to build something from the ground up."

Radi Jarai, a professor in his sixties at Al-Quds University, listens to everyone. He is a one-state proponent and no longer believes in any two-state model. He talks about the refugees' right to return to their homes. Some of the people in the room are from families who were exiled in 1948. Awni's family, for example, was deported from the village of Al-Qabu, near what is today the Jewish community of Mevo Beitar. The village well-spring, now located in Menachem Begin Park, is named Ein Kobi—a derivation from the Arabic "Qabu." Awni was born in 1953, and his childhood years were tough, with constant changes; nowhere was home because they believed they would be going home soon. The late writer Salman Natour wrote about the second generation of the Nakba:

> We were all born with the Nakba and were therefore destined, against our will, to become witnesses. We became carriers of testimony, not because we had seen the horrors of it, but because we had heard about them from our predecessors...We were born after the war, yet we are obliged to carry its weight and burden...We love this tale about our lost childhood. We love to say that we sacrificed our childhood for a noble cause.[3]

Although the plan is to discuss our draft statement, the conversation meanders into broader topics, as it always does. One of

---

3 From "The Chronicle of the Wrinkled-Face Sheikh" by Salman Natour. *Granta Israel 1* (November 2014), translated by Yehouda Shenhav-Shaharabani.

the Israelis says that most of the houses Radi is talking about no longer exist, and those that do have new inhabitants—if you try to remove them from their homes in favor of the refugees, they will fight back. Radi suggests a different approach: the exiled Palestinian landlords will rent their homes to the Israelis currently living in them. "But there are many places Palestinians were deported from where no one is living now. Why couldn't the refugees go back there?" He says this not defiantly, but truly seeking to understand why the idea is impossible for Israelis to accept. One of the Israelis says it's an untenable plan because things have changed in the intervening decades, villages have vanished and towns have sprung up, you can't right one wrong with another and expect to suddenly alter Israel's character. Besides, they point out, show us a precedent for millions of refugees returning after seventy years to homes that no longer exist.

"The question is not whether it's ever happened before," Radi replies. "After all, up until World War Two there had never been that kind of event. The question is what solution can be offered to the refugees."

I ask why the right to return to a Palestinian state, assuming one comes into existence, would not satisfy him, with added compensation for stolen property.

"Because those aren't their lands," he explains. "And if we're talking about compensation, have you ever asked yourself how much money the State of Israel owes the Palestinians for the property stolen in 1948? Houses, fields, agricultural equipment, everything? How can it be that you don't even discuss this in Israel?"

Radi and I smoke cigarettes by the office window and look out onto the tiled rooftops of the houses in Psagot, a settlement not even a mile away from us, with its houses perched high above the surrounding Arab communities in typical settlement-style. About three hundred families live in Psagot. Not one of the people in the room has ever visited there. "How much longer do you think that place is going to sit there looking down on me?" Radi wonders.

Al-Beiruti, who is retired from a job in the Palestinian security apparatus, has white curly hair and the air of an absent-minded professor. He's tired of talking politics. He tells us he's started growing dates at his home in Jericho. "It's a new *muba-dara*," he murmurs—a new initiative. I don't know whether or not to believe him; he often adopts a look of bemused irony and it's hard to tell when he's joking.

***

In the imposing Fatah building, my three Israeli colleagues and I are welcomed by Muhammad al-Madani's sharply dressed young aides. They've done their research on us: "I don't think there is a 'world shadow,'" one of them comments in reference to the title of my latest novel, and he wishes one of the other Israelis a happy birthday. We sit in a circle. Al-Madani, also white-haired, with a gray moustache and a soft voice, is frequently called to the phone or to review a document. Our Palestinian-Jewish group presents him with our initiative: "We see a shared homeland in the expanse between the Jordan River and the Mediterranean, which both peoples are intricately connected to through their historical and religious memory. Within this shared homeland, the two peoples will fulfill their national aspirations by means of two independent sovereign states, with recognized borders based on the borders of 4 June, 1967. The borders between the two states will be open, and the citizens of both states will have freedom of movement and residence throughout the homeland." The main tenets of the initiative are no separation between Jews and Palestinians, no one removed from his home, the right for everyone to move throughout the entire space, and both peoples realizing their national aspirations within their respective states.

One member of the group explains that the notion of two states, of separation, is dead—the Jewish and Palestinian populations are too intermingled. One of the Palestinians adds: "A lot of politicians and diplomats, at least publicly, express certainty that the implementation of two states based on the classic formula is a matter of time. They've seen for decades, mostly because of settlement construction, that the vision is losing its relevance to the changing geography, yet still they believe that some unnamed rational force will lead us there."

Al-Madani does not like these last comments. He believes that two states, based on international parameters, is the only possible formula; after all, greater changes have occurred in history. "Your proposal might be relevant at a later stage," he responds. "The Palestinians don't want separation anyway. But right now there are parameters accepted by the international community regarding the two-state solution, and we will implement them first of all." His answer comes as no surprise: PA representatives and affiliated journalists always present the official position, even when they may be saying something different between the lines. They repeatedly refer to "the international community's parameters." Still, when you talk to different groups of people in Palestinian cities, you hear less about a Palestinian state and the international community, and more about "freedom of movement," the checkpoints, prisoners, arrests, frustration at being unable to meet relatives in Nazareth or visit East Jerusalem. And you hear about the refugees.

From the window we can see buildings and cranes, blue sky and heaps of trash. One of the Israelis says it's impossible to make progress because the Israelis are not desperate but merely indifferent, while the Palestinians are not indifferent but desperate. Al-Madani is frustrated by Israeli apathy, and asks why the Israeli left does not make its voice heard on the issue of prisoners and the occupation. Only in Ramallah would anyone still expect forcefulness from the Israeli left. Israelis claim the public is uninterested in prisoners or in negotiations. Al-Madani seems to understand the situation, but struggles to accept how it could be so.

We move to a conference room for lunch. I sit down next to one of al-Madani's aides, a young man in a suit who has a master's degree from Tel Aviv University and is considering pursuing his doctoral studies there. We talk about Palestinians who see Ramallah as an alienating, cold city. He says his parents don't come near Ramallah, not even to visit him. One of the people at the table used to be a journalist in Israel and lived in the north of the country. After the Second Intifada he moved to Ramallah because he could no longer tolerate the propaganda in the Israeli media: he would file reports on Palestinians killed in the territories, sometimes dozens of them, and nothing would be published. Finally he realized these stories didn't interest anyone.

The aide seated on my other side is a shy young man whom I barely noticed at first. I overhear him telling another guest that he recently got out of an Israeli prison after an eight-year term. Many of his friends had been killed in the Second Intifada. There were scores of Palestinian casualties not far from these offices, by the military headquarters of the IDF's Judea & Samaria Division. One day he couldn't take it anymore, so he picked up a rifle and went out to shoot Jews. One of his bullets hit an Arab Israeli, who fortunately was not killed, and he spent a few years in prison. After he got out he made up his mind he was through with violence, or at least that he'd paid his debt to the violent struggle. He now works in al-Madani's office. Someone tells him he looks like an eighteen-year-old kid, and he blushes. It's hard to reconcile his appearance with the story: his entire demeanor says star pupil.

Outside, I think back to my first visit to Ramallah. It was in the summer of 2000, on an extremely hot day, about a month before the Camp David summit and the beginning of the Second Intifada. I was twenty-three years old, accompanying my father (a member of Knesset at the time) and a group of other politicians, including Knesset member Ahmed Tibi, on a visit to Arafat's headquarters, known as the Mukata'a. Ramallah looked lovely and quiet as I gazed out of the car window, and I swallowed up the scenes hungrily, staring at the different license plates, at the Palestinian police officers' uniforms, at the cranes swinging above us. At the Mukata'a we were welcomed by Yasser Arafat in his green uniform. He spoke firmly at the meeting, saying he could not fathom why it was so urgent to convene a summit at Camp David. The Americans were pressuring him to go because the Israeli prime minister Ehud Barak was pressuring them, but he didn't understand the hurry and saw no evidence that the sides were in agreement. When asked what his demands were, he replied: A Palestinian state within the '67 borders, including East Jerusalem, and a solution to the refugee problem. At the end of the meeting we moved to a room where a long table was set for lunch. They sat me next to Arafat himself, who softened now, smiled a lot and poked at his food without really eating. After a while he handed me kibbeh and cubes of kebab from his own plate.

* * *

A few weeks after our meeting with Al-Madani, I visit Ramallah again. It's less bustling now, on this summer day in 2014, and everything has changed again in the interim: three Jewish boys were kidnapped earlier this month and are still missing. The army is searching for them, arresting Hamas members in the West Bank as part of a campaign named Operation Brother's Keeper. We stop at a building with a shattered front window. Passersby grind large shards of glass under their shoes on the sidewalk, and the sound rings through the street. The people gathered outside the building do not believe the Jewish boys were kidnapped by Palestinians. They think the kids just went down to the resort city of Eilat for some fun, and the whole story was fabricated by Israel as a pretext to re-arrest the prisoners it let go in return for the kidnapped soldier Gilad Shalit.

Inside, we take the elevator to the third floor, where several offices stand empty and the dark hallways are deserted. The walls of a spacious suite are decorated with glossy white signs emblazoned with the word "Progress," the company's name, and a list of courses it offers. On a table in the small lobby is a stack of newspapers, topped with the weekend supplements of the Israeli newspapers. Sounds of electronic music reach us from somewhere nearby.

Progress is a new language school that teaches mostly Hebrew. The founding partners are seated in the director's office. All three are Hamas members who served long stints in Israeli prisons and got out in the past few years. I ask why they were arrested, and, much like the Fatah men I spoke with a few weeks ago, they signal for me to change the subject. They say they are no longer in Hamas, not involved in any organization, just running the school. But Israeli soldiers recently came by to question them; evidence of their visit can be seen in the bent handle on the front door and the shattered windows downstairs. This is another group of men who spent a long time in prison and are trying to rebuild their lives, start families, establish themselves financially. Not all of them are willing to be photographed. Their main fear is that the army will arrest them again, and if that were to happen there is no telling when they would get out—it could be two months or a year. Everything they've built since getting out, including their cherished private business, could collapse.

The school director, Jalal Rumana, lounges in an armchair behind his desk, emitting puffs of cigarette smoke, and greets us in a booming voice. He is an amputee and his body is almost entirely covered with burn scars. "Workplace accident," he scoffs when I enquire. In 1998, Rumana planned to detonate a car bomb in downtown Jerusalem, but the car caught fire while he was still in it. He suffered severe burns, and spent months in hospital and another fifteen years in an Israeli prison. He stands up ceremoniously, walks over to a bureau and shows me an ornately framed certificate: a master's degree in interdisciplinary studies from Israel's Open University. "I know all the books by Benny Morris, Shlomo Avineri, Zeev Sternhell and the Israel Democracy Institute," he brags. Indeed, Rumana is proficient in the ideas of Zionism and the intricacies of Israeli politics. He can quote from religious rulings handed down by the Jewish spiritual authority Ovadia Yosef, and from the writings of Ahad Ha'am, a prominent pre-state Zionist essayist. He discusses the integration of Russian immigrants in Israel. He is sometimes interviewed about Israelis on al-Aqsa TV. He has an ironic expression, and his smile sometimes seems to be saying: Come on, you're not going to tell me anything about the Israelis that I don't already know. He talks excitedly about a book he wrote in prison, in Arabic, entitled *Zionism, Where to?* "My research is based only on Israeli sources, and my hypothesis is that Zionism peaked in 1967 and since then it's been in decline. There have only been withdrawals—from Yamit in the Sinai, from Lebanon, from Gaza, and there was also a plan to withdraw from the West Bank. In the future, the Zionist project will withdraw from the Triangle[4] and other places, and the end is clear."

I ask if he would be willing to have the book translated into Hebrew.

"I would like that very much. And although I'm no longer in Hamas, I will call it: *The Conflict as Seen by Hamas*. Nir, can you do something about it? Maybe it'll be a joint *mubadara* by the two of us." He laughs.

I hedge: "I'm not sure, it's hard to do well with books now—the whole industry is a mess."

"Then we'll sell it on the internet," he suggests.

"What is your view on Zionism?" I ask.

"I acknowledge the Jewish problem in the twentieth century. I acknowledge the persecutions, and the Holocaust led by the great criminal Hitler. I have sympathy for the Jews, but, after all, Jews like Moses Mendelssohn were French or German. They lived in the West, and they got taken in by Zionism, and that's why the Jews adopted a secular ideology that was incompatible with their religious tradition. The Jews' problems were in the

---

4 A cluster of towns and villages in northern Israel, adjacent to the Green Line, and home to Israel's largest concentration of Arab citizens.

West, not in the East, and in the West is where they should solve them."

"So I presume neither two states nor a binational state is the solution in your opinion?"

"Even if there were two states within the '67 borders, no Palestinian would truly accept that. Because where is the right of return? Where is my home? And if there is a right of return, there won't be any Zionism anyway."

"What rights do Jews have in this expanse?"

"The Jewish state was founded on the home of my mother, who was driven from Lod in 1948. You were dispossessed, and you used the evil and dispossession inflicted on you against my family and my people. The Jews' political resolution is not here. We have to recognize together that the Jews will reintegrate into the societies they came from: France, Germany, Britain and, of course, Russia."

"My grandfather came from Aden, in Yemen," I point out. "Assuming he were still alive, where would he and millions of other Middle Eastern Jews return to?"

"The Jews can't go back to Arab states, I don't want them to suffer. So they'll return to a third state. It's not a punishment: as soon as Poland got into the EU, every Israeli with half a Polish document was running to the embassy for a passport, and now it's the same with Spain. Maybe the Jews also know this isn't going to last."

"Why deny Jews the right to be citizens? That is what is being done to the Palestinians, after all, isn't it?"

"In my opinion, all due respect goes to Herzl, who said: We'll come to this place, and if the Arabs agree we'll have a homeland. But that isn't what you did. In my years in prison I didn't change my views, but I did change my opinion about what means we should use, and so I say: despite Sabra and Shatila and Deir Yassin and other massacres, and the thousands of casualties, and the children who were murdered, and the checkpoints, I don't want a drop of blood spilled either from my people or from the Jews. There is no point in the Jews staying on as a minority in a Palestinian state. There is too much hostility."

"So you want to convince more than six million Jews, many of whom did not come from Europe, that the solution is for them to emigrate to Europe?"

"If Jews had come here in the forties as refugees, I would have hosted them warmly in my home. But you didn't do that, did you? You came in with full force, including international force. I know there are many clever Jews with good hearts, but they have to understand that the Palestinians have paid the whole price for your past, and there is no solution except for the Jews to go back to the countries they came from, and for everyone to fulfill their rights in their own countries."

He speaks eagerly, as if genuinely hoping to convince me, and suggests that after he publishes his book in Hebrew we travel to Jerusalem together so that he can lecture at the Hebrew University. "I'm prepared for the criticism," he notes.

"You understand you're not really leaving the Jews any options here?"

"Human beings who believe in humanity must discard ideas that cause injustice, like the occupation and Zionism. I want you all to know: you have caused a second Holocaust for the Palestinian people. And look, if you stay here, with your Zionism and your clout, there will never be peace, Nir, and the future victims will be your brother or my mother, and I don't want any more people to die."

"Where are you willing to compromise?"

"Listen, I respect the Jewish religion, where they say that you will return to the Land of Israel when the Messiah comes, right? I'm a Muslim and I also believe in the Messiah, and I'm telling you: go back to Europe, and in the future the Messiah can decide our case."

* * *

About a hundred students are signed up at the language school, mostly women. They file in, women in hijab, kids with backpacks, young mothers and one middle-aged man.

"Why are you learning Hebrew?" I ask a young woman from Bir Nabala, in English.

"I work with Hebrew documents at a law firm in Ramallah," she explains.

In one classroom they are studying the Hebrew alphabet, and the other is silent as students take their final exam. A young partner who is not currently teaching leans against the wall in a handsome suit, his hair neatly slicked back, with a trim beard.

He served eight years in prison. There, like Rumana, he learned Hebrew, and earned undergraduate and graduate degrees. He is currently preparing to write a doctoral dissertation about women's political rights in Islam.

We stand in the hallway talking softly, while I smoke a cigarette. He prefers me not to mention his name. He quit smoking, doesn't drink alcohol or coffee, and runs every morning. I immediately feel ungainly and ill. He is twenty-nine and has two kids, an eight-year-old boy and a four-year-old girl. "First thing after I got out of prison, I married a family friend. Now I'm managing this place and also teaching at a school. You could say that of the three partners, I'm responsible for the business side. In prison you have to decide if you're just going to let the time pass, or take advantage of it," he says. "I decided to own my time: I prepared myself for the day I got out of prison."

I ask about the school's business model.

"We teach everything ourselves and charge each student four hundred shekels (about US$100). At first we only taught languages, but recently we've expanded. We teach Arabic and math for matriculation too. It's called *mubadara*, which means initiative." He smiles and talks about the dissertation he may write. He is toying with the idea of studying in England. We hear a drumbeat from outside the office suite again. "The company next door is a very different business," he says.

I ask if he agrees with Rumana's solution.

"Maybe theoretically, on the analytical level," he answers unenthusiastically, "but practically it has no chance. If I take a sober look at things, there is no solution to the conflict at present. I'm not even talking about politics—how much of that can we do?" He's hinting at his distaste for Rumana's unfettered talk, or perhaps he's saying something else: I'm not talking politics *with you*, certainly not now. The Israeli army's operation in the West Bank is still underway, soldiers raided these offices only a few days ago, and he clearly fears arrest.

Meanwhile words in Hebrew come from the classroom: *beit sefer*—school, *ir*—city, *medina*—country. Jalal Rumana asks in Hebrew: *"Eifo atem garim?"* (Where do you live?) All the women answer: "Ramallah."

"After twenty-five hours they're already writing Hebrew," the teacher says proudly. The girls in this classroom are dressed differently. In the first row sits a young woman wearing a colorful floral jellabiya over a yellow blouse and jeans. Her fingernails and toenails are painted red and blue. Next to her sits a skinny boy with curly hair in a blue tracksuit. He is the class star. "We live in Palestine," he answers in Hebrew. I ask how many of his friends speak Hebrew. "None of them," he replies. We've evened out now, I realize: it used to be that a majority of West Bank Palestinians, who worked in Israel, spoke Hebrew and Arabic, while Jews only knew Hebrew. But now the younger generation of Jews speak no Arabic and the Palestinians don't know any Hebrew.

The young partner explains that most of the students are learning Hebrew not for a love of the language, but because they need it for their jobs. He introduces me to a student who is a resident of Israel, from Kafr 'Aqab on the outskirts of Jerusalem. She is twenty-seven, and has worked for a few years at the Standards Institution of Israel. "I want to move up to a more senior position," she explains. "It's time. And without Hebrew it'll be difficult, although I would prefer to learn French."

We step out into the hallway, and the electronic music gets louder. In the doorway to the office next to the school, a young woman with long hair and wearing a black dress kicks around a small toy truck with her bare feet, while two stylishly dressed young men stand next to her. This suite is a music recording business. We talk in English, which they speak fluently, and they invite us into the studio. They record music mostly by young artists, some Arabic pop, and sometimes more traditional music. They play us songs by musicians from Gaza, Alexandria and elsewhere. The studio is this young group's *mubadara*, and they seem upbeat: "There's lots of work, even in the past couple of weeks."

They are aware that the army was in the building last week, but they don't talk politics much. Unlike the language school's directors, who have spent most of their lives in conflict with the occupation regime whether they liked it or not, these young people's contact with Israelis (including the army) has been minimal, confined mostly to the checkpoints. They aren't as interested in Israelis as the older generation, forgoing the analysis of Israeli society and its positions on the conflict. Their formative years were spent in a post-Oslo Ramallah. They have never worked in Israel and all say they've never visited Tel Aviv or West Jerusalem and feel no urgent need to do so. Their cultural space, one of them tells me, is the Arab world, and also music from Europe, especially France. They converse with me as though I were a guest from a foreign country taking an interest in their music, and they never use the plural "you" that is so often addressed to Israelis as representatives of the occupying entity.

I wonder if their indifference to our Israeliness is demonstrative, or if I'm just feeling out of place and searching for a similar feeling in them. Perhaps the only thing in their behavior that gives away the fact that there are Israeli forces out there who could affect their lives is their refusal to talk to me about the IDF's operation in the West Bank. I'm unsure whether their avoidance of politics stems from cautiousness or if they're just tired of rehashing the obvious. Perhaps a little of both. The Gazan singer's track they play seems to assault me from all directions inside the studio. Writers often envy the simplicity with which musicians dazzle their listeners, employing that unspoken essence found only in music; it's impossible to explain why a particular combination of notes is so exciting. For a couple of moments, we all stand with our eyes closed, listening to the music.

* * *

On the street outside the building with the broken windows, the group that welcomed us in the morning gathers again. We talk about recent events. A little boy in a red Liverpool T-shirt walks past and hears us talking. He stops. *"Inte Yahudi?"* he asks with a strange glint in his eyes. "Are you Jewish?" he repeats, his expression curious. I nod. He shakes his head in disbelief. "He's Jewish?" he asks the crowd around us in Arabic. One of the older Palestinians explains: the boy has never seen a Jew before. "He's always hearing about Jews, but you're the first Jew he's ever seen in his life."

4

I See Gaza
from My Window
Kibbutz Nirim

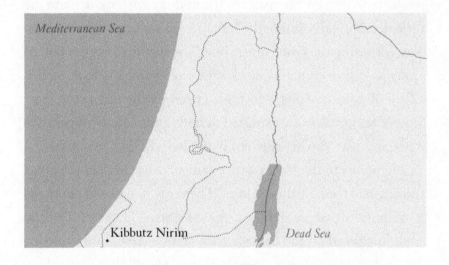

Mediterranean Sea

Kibbutz Nirim

Dead Sea

Two boys play tennis on the courts on the edge of Kibbutz Nirim beneath a perfectly blue sky. They wear shorts and brightly colored T-shirts, and their shouts can be heard from a distance. Suddenly there is an engine roar and, after a minute or two of tense expectation, tanks lurch toward the tennis court, kicking up dirt, and the boys disappear behind a cloud of dust. When the tanks are gone and the dust begins to settle, they come back into view: one of them runs to the net, swings his racket up high and almost vanishes behind the remaining yellow cloud.

It's the summer of 2014, and the tanks have been a fixture on the kibbutz landscape since Operation Protective Edge, Israel's military campaign against Hamas-ruled Gaza, began about three weeks ago. There is local unease with the army's conduct. While most public discourse in Israel is busy boosting the IDF, championing its accomplishments and heroics, some of Nirim's residents are less enthusiastic. In the midday heat, we drive to the agricultural fields outside the kibbutz with a few kibbutz members, including the crops supervisor. The dirt road is engulfed in a grayish-yellow grime—"Tank dust," he grumbles. To our left is a field of peanut plants, which are currently the main crop here. Most of the peanuts are exported to Italy, although the supervisor is perplexed as to why; apparently the Italians love peanuts.

He points to the places where tanks have trampled the crops and crushed the irrigation hoses. "The army has caused hundreds of millions' worth of damage," he laments. "They've killed the land. Just based on the damage they've done here, I can imagine the kind of things they're doing in Gaza." He tells me angrily how a group of paratroopers turned up outside the kibbutz one night. They'd come from the Gaza Strip, exhausted from warfare, and the army bus had just dropped them off near the kibbutz's back fence without telling anyone they'd be arriving.

We stand at the edge of the farming lands, gazing at a row of buildings a mile away: the outskirts of the Gaza Strip. Beyond a row of trees is the village of Khuza'a, or as it's known

in Arabic, Khirbat Ikhzaa, which echoes the name of a famous
novella by the Israeli author S. Yizhar about the depopulation of
a Palestinian village in the war of 1948. (Yizhar published his
novella *Khirbet Khizeh* in Hebrew in 1949, and it has recently
appeared in an English translation.) In fact, Yizhar modelled his
story on a different village, near what is today Ashkelon.

The billowing dust on the horizon attests to Israeli tanks
on the move. "We'll go see a tunnel now," says the supervisor,
displaying enthusiasm for the first time. The tunnel is famous
around the kibbutz. Braver members, like Peter, the swimming-
pool lifeguard, have even walked through it (as did, it turns out,
a few government ministers). Our chaperones point to some dust
clouds about seven hundred yards away: that's where the tunnel
is. But all I can make out are two fig trees. Someone says there
are actually three. Dust clouds? No, fig trees. The tunnel is surrounded by glistening green fields.

The tunnel was exposed about six months before the war.
One day an IDF division commander came to Nirim, convened
the kibbutz emergency teams and informed them that a tunnel
had been discovered, but not to worry, the army was protecting
them.

"If you've uncovered tunnels," someone asked, "and terrorists
might emerge from them, then why is the entire army set up to
observe the Gaza Strip instead of the kibbutz?"

"Excellent question," the commander responded. "There's no
budget for that."

We pass fields of watermelons, yams, avocados and empty

chicken coops. "Want to see a Qassam rocket?" they ask. Not wanting to disappoint my hosts, I nod. We search for the rocket among the yams ("they're grown on the kibbutz from A to Z, including sales"), but the Qassam has perplexingly disappeared.

The crops supervisor and a young man who works with him are careful to draw a distinction between their own criticism of the army, which stems from their location in Israel's so-called "periphery" (a term commonly used in Israeli discourse to label any area outside the major cities), and that voiced by the Tel Aviv left wing. Someone whispers that even on Alumim and Sa'ad (two religious kibbutzim nearby), "where the army is God, there is sharp criticism of it." We go back to the main kibbutz area. Next to the gate we stop by a truck full of Asian foreign workers, who have just come back from planting avocados. They sit crowded in the back wearing thin black clothing, their faces covered with black scarves, with only their eyes visible.

Night falls on Nirim. It's quiet here, and not a soul is out on the paths. After days of bombardments, a ceasefire was declared, but it expires tomorrow at midnight. Some of the kibbutz members who left during the worst of the bombings have come back, but they know fighting may resume tomorrow night. The only place I find anyone out and about is on the plaza outside the youth clubhouse. Teenaged boys and girls sprawl on chairs, benches and swings, some of them smoking, and proudly show off the beers they can easily get hold of. They're in high spirits. These kids, aged thirteen to fifteen, are reconvening after weeks during which the kibbutz was shelled and they scattered to various places around Israel and the world. Liav spent two weeks in Holland and Belgium, Ofir was on Mishmar Ha'Emek, a kibbutz in northern Israel that took in many members of Nirim, Yair (one of the tennis players) went to Germany and Kfar Saba.

They invite us into their club, a three-room apartment with a pool table in one room, a ping-pong table in another, and one large room with couches and a wide-screen TV. After I lose a game of ping-pong to one of the boys, we gather in the TV room. They all came back to Nirim when the ceasefire was announced, but are prepared to evacuate again if fighting is renewed. "Every war, we head off somewhere else," one of them says. His family moved to Nirim from Kfar Saba because his parents wanted a kibbutz education for their kids. "All the kibbutz members here are lefties," he says, "but I'm not. I'm not willing to sacrifice anything for the Palestinians. They can live under our rule. If they don't want to, there are twenty-one other states. I mean, if the rockets landing here were landing in Tel Aviv, they'd have wiped out Gaza by now. In Tel Aviv if you hear a siren, you can get up, you can get dressed, all that. Here, you don't hear a siren—you hear a whistle."

One boy tells of a mortar bomb that landed in the driveway of his house. There was no air-raid siren: he heard the ominous whistle, then a massive explosion. The window in his bedroom shattered. Everyone quickly digs through their cell phones and, with the enthusiasm of veteran soldiers recollecting the glory of past battles, they show me pictures of mortars: on fields, on the path to the swimming pool, on a strip of lawn. They compete over who was in the greatest danger, and have evolved their own rules for coping with the sirens. "Whenever you hear 'Red Color' but you don't hear a whistle, everything's fine. If you hear a whistle, run like your life depended on it." 'Red Color' is the code broadcast by the emergency missile-warning system.

I tell them I've heard from people on the kibbutz who are desperate and want to leave. They reply unanimously that they don't want to live in the city, they prefer a kibbutz or moshav. There are kids from different backgrounds here: some are third-generation kibbutz members, others moved here with their parents and a few were adopted by kibbutz families. Liav, for example, was born in Bat Yam near Tel Aviv, Ofir was born in Lod, and another boy was born in Kfar Saba. The ratio of Ashkenazis to Mizrahis is different among the kids from the rest of the kibbutz, with a roughly even split. The military security co-ordinator's son walks in; he knows about strategic affairs, the other kids say. The discussion turns to the tunnels, a topical fear.

Liav is convinced there's a tunnel under her house. A few years ago she heard drilling and digging sounds from underground. She would put her ear against the floor and hear cell phones ringing. Her parents notified the army, and soldiers came over with some kind of machine and said they couldn't find anything. A few of the kids don't believe her story.

Casually tossing around names of operations like "Cast Lead" and "Pillar of Defense," these kids seem to have cultivated their own private war-language that includes types of rockets, what to do when you're being shot at, army units, and memorable events like the massive mushroom cloud over Gaza during "Pillar of Defense," after the assassination of a senior Hamas member. "They don't tell you everything," one boy assures me. "We know about strikes you don't even hear about."

I tell them there are quite a lot of left-wingers on the kibbutz. Are any of them on the left?

No! They all seem horrified by my question. "You can't live here and be a lefty," they decree. "The media is leftist, that's why the war only started after they shot at Tel Aviv. When they only shoot at us, no one cares." They mock the left wing's anti-war demonstrations in Tel Aviv. "I support all the Arabs getting the hell out of our faces forever," says one boy. "I can identify with that," his friend says.

But Liav disagrees. "People in Gaza are experiencing worse things than we are here," she says. "If I'd been born on the other side, I'd be in Hamas," someone offers. "The second we turned up in Israel we took over everything they had." The son of a long-time kibbutz family says, "We can wipe out Gaza, but maybe we can't kill everyone there. Anyway, we should give a big fuck-you to the UN."

Everyone knows the ceasefire will expire tomorrow at midnight and they may not be here the day after that, but for now they enjoy their time together. As the debate draws on, it turns out that their political affiliations are not along the lines of oldtimers versus newbies, or Mizrahis versus Ashkenazis, but rather follow a gender division. Adopting the local vernacular, one could say that the girls tend to be "lefties."

I ask if I can put a slightly provocative question to them. I'd like their response to a report I read out loud to them:

In the bombing of a residential building in Khan Yunis on 29 July, the following people were killed: Omar Wadah Hassan Abu 'Amer, aged twelve; 'Abd al-Ghani Wadah Hassan Abu 'Amer, aged ten; 'Imad Wadah Hassan Abu 'Amer, aged nine; 'Issa Wadah Hassan Abu 'Amer, aged seven; 'Iz a-Din Wadah Hassan Abu 'Amer, aged five; Muhammad Ahmad Suliman Abu 'Amer, aged eleven.

The kids respond:

"They're children and they didn't do anything wrong, but they'll grow up and be *shaheeds*.[5] If they bombed that place, there must have been a reason."

"There's a justification, of course. You know how they said the IDF shot at children on the beach in Gaza for no reason? Turns out kids were firing rockets on Israel."

"The IDF gives warnings before they bomb. They can choose to take it seriously or not."

"Ninety-five percent of them will be terrorists. They learn to hate Jews in school."

"The IDF is the most moral army in the world."

---

5 The Arabic term for "martyr," commonly used as an honorific for Muslims who die in the cause of *jihad* or protest, or who are killed by Israeli forces.

"It's hard for me to hear these things," Liav says. "There's someone there exactly like you, a child who wants to live and wants to have fun and wants happiness. Like you."

"But there's no choice!" one boy yells.

"Then kill them, I just don't want to know about it," Liav concedes wearily.

* * *

A few distinct groups emerged in Nirim during the weeks of war: the children left, usually with their young parents; some people in their forties left while some stayed; and the old-time kibbutz members all stayed. One thing gradually becomes clear: in my conversations with the older generation, the war is not the issue. They've seen bigger ones, after all, and they are more concerned with other topics—one in particular. If you spent a whole day with the kibbutz kids you would probably never hear about it, but for the older people it is more worrying and wounding than the war. Our visit to Nirim coincided with the aftermath of a huge struggle, and the first person to mention it was Moshe Etzion.

I met him early one morning next to the auto shop. Etzion has been a kibbutz member for forty years, which means he was not one of the founders. He was born in Tehran and was in the first graduating class of the Max Fein Technological College in Tel Aviv. He came to Nirim in 1970, when they were looking for a technician to set up an irrigation system on the fields near the border, where members were forbidden to go because of frequent incursions by the *Fedayeen* (Palestinian guerrillas who infiltrated Israel from neighboring Arab states, starting in the early 1950s, to attack military and civilian targets, mostly near the borders). He is the father of the military security co-ordinator on the kibbutz, whose son we met earlier at the club.

"I came to the kibbutz with big ideas," Etzion recalls. "I wanted a real kibbutz. In recent years there's been a privatization process underway here. I opposed the privatization, both ideologically and personally. But, as time went by I saw that the younger generation wanted it, including my son, and so I decided to co-operate. Unfortunately, in the future Nirim will look more like a regular village."

I ask him about the future of Nirim; people seem to have given up on the idea of a peaceful life here.

"The Palestinians want to kick us out," he says, "because the Arab entity has not come to terms with our existence. I hope they won't succeed. But we have to talk with them and decide on clear borders. Nirim will survive, everyone will come back when the fighting dies down. This is a kibbutz where most of the members are active, our economic condition is good, and that attracts people. In my opinion, out of all those threatening to leave, no one actually will. Since I left the city I haven't regretted it even once."

In the home of Gila and Haim Shilo there is a large bookcase lined with novels, botanical guides, and issues of the Eshkol Regional Council newsletter ("Why are there so many flies in Eshkol and what can be done about it?" a recent headline asks).

This house acts as the kibbutz's informal library during the war. People who are afraid to walk around outside come here to exchange books. Like most of the old-timers, the Shilos have not left, and they sleep in a *Mamad* (the Hebrew acronym for "Residential Secure Space," a reinforced room required by Israeli law in all residential structures) furnished with a bed, armchair and television. Their four children have left the kibbutz for cities, villages, or other communities that do not follow a co-operative model. I ask the couple whether they view this as a failure, and they concede that their children's decisions to leave saddened them.

Gila and Haim are proud of being the longest-standing members of the kibbutz today. At twenty, while he was working at a flour mill in Tel Aviv, Haim joined a youth group that became the founding core of Nirim. Right after Yom Kippur in 1946, in an operation code-named "The 11-Point Aliya," eleven communities were founded in the northern Negev, including Dangour, where the core group lived initially. During the '48 war the Egyptian army bombed Dangour heavily and the community suffered a fatal blow. Haim tells how all the buildings were destroyed, except one wall in the dining-room hut, on which they wrote the slogan: "The victor will not be the tank, but man." After the war, the group sought out a new place to live. Haim recalls: "What did we look for? Wherever the wheat grew high, that's where we wanted to be." In 1949, Kibbutz Nirim was founded.

The Shilos immediately tell me about the white house near the kibbutz, which belonged to the Abu Sita family, an Arab family of Bedouin origin that controlled a large swath of land in the area and was deported or fled in '48. Now they live in Gaza. "We put down roots here, but they had a home here, too, and I always remember that," says Gila. They also make a point of mentioning the ancient Jewish ties to the place, as evidenced by the sixth-century Maon Synagogue, which was uncovered at an adjacent archeological site.

Haim and Gila had various jobs on the kibbutz: he hauled sacks of flour, ran a shoe factory and then an electronics plant. She worked as a librarian and at the plant nursery, and helped build the fence around the kibbutz. They've been here for seventy years and can't remember all the things they've done. They were loyal members who always put the kibbutz's needs first. Gila feels that when those needs conflicted with her individual views, she always acceded, and something in her personality was not given rein to express itself. She says she is at peace with the price she paid. "The togetherness gave people a lot of strength to overcome the many obstacles."

But the big change, a crisis which left them with wounds that may never heal, occurred only recently: privatization. Unlike Moshe Etzion, they have not come to terms with it at all. "Before privatization, the kibbutz had a creative spirit," Gila explains, "and I liked life here. The big conflict over privatization was very difficult for us. These ideas are in complete opposition to the way we lived, and there were bitter arguments, with shouting and fighting between parents and children." She pauses for a moment to choose her words carefully. "I experienced a mourning period after the decision to privatize. Afterwards, I decided I would not dwell on it anymore and I stopped coming to kibbutz meetings."

Haim said it's no longer the kibbutz they wanted and founded, and the crisis is profound. They both believe that the new system leaves each to his own, and that, whereas in the past the kibbutz was based on mutual aid and responsibility, those values are no longer part of the kibbutz ethos. "The idea of privatization came from people in their forties and fifties who wanted more economic freedom, but it created a different kibbutz." Gila emphasizes that she understands it's the young people's turn to choose their lifestyles now. "We've already lived our lives." Of course there were problems with the collective model, they concede. For example, there were people who didn't work enough. But today, in the privatized system, it's the weak who pay the price. "Suddenly a family with three kids can't survive in Nirim on a ten-thousand-shekel salary. That is inconceivable."

"You've lived here for seventy years," I say. "The place has grown and become well established, but you've witnessed constant wars and military operations. You still talk like leftists, but perhaps in your hearts you sense despair. In 1948 your community was destroyed, whole Arab villages were devastated right in front of you, and here you are almost seven decades later and again we are in the throes of war."

"Our viewpoint has not changed. We're here because we have to settle the land," says Gila, "but, since coming here, things have only deteriorated. The children used to be able to go out around the *wadi* on their own, and we would meet Gazans on a daily basis. Today the children need a chaperone everywhere they go, and the only Gazans we see are dead, on television. In this operation I had no doubt that all the children had to leave, but I think back to 1956, when Dayan sent troops here and provoked the Egyptians and there were canons lined up by the avocados and they shot over our heads from the Gaza Strip, and I was in charge of the children in the nursery and I would plan how to take them down to the bomb shelter. Today I wonder what sort of world these children are growing up into."

"The population used to be homogenous here," Haim adds. "Today there are people who come for all sorts of reasons, including profitability. On the one hand these people aren't willing to live on the kibbutz without one hundred percent security, on the other hand life is good here for them and so many people want to come, and I think they will want to come after the war too."

I ask if they support the operation in Gaza.

"We have the right to defend ourselves, but there is no justification for hundreds of children being killed in Gaza," Haim replies. "The devastation we have caused there is intolerable. And the world is watching."

"So are you troubled by our reflection in the mirror, or our image in the world?"

"Both," he answers candidly.

"The population there is held hostage by Hamas," says Gila. "It breaks my heart to see the devastation and suffering. You asked about failure: all my life I believed in peace and I lived in this place, and now here I am at this old age and again we are at war. But I don't feel a sense of failure. I know we haven't wasted our lives. We did what we believed in."

* * *

Everyone is awaiting the midnight hour, when the ceasefire will expire. On one path we meet two young girls who immediately tell us about their media appearance in the weekend supplement of a major daily newspaper. "We were on the cover of *24 Hours!*" they boast, and insist that our photographer take their picture. Everyone on this kibbutz is well aware of the role they play in the public eye. Quite a few kids maintain portfolios of press clippings, and others have their media appearances filed away in their parents' memories. One mother hugs her little boy and rattles off his resume: "He was on Channel 2 News, on *New Evening*, and on a special show on the Children's Channel before the music festival." The adults may not celebrate their own media appearances openly, but they also drop references. One woman has a blog where she corresponds with a girl in Gaza, another was on CNN. Nirim seems to comprise two entities: the kibbutz where ordinary people live while bombs fall around them, and at the same time its own self-conscious representation. A sort of war tourism has evolved here. I keep meeting members who want to show me mortar shrapnel damage that only they know about, on the walls of their homes, or even on trees.

Arnon Avni, the architect of the privatization plan, is the nemesis of Nirim's old-timers, and it's no coincidence that he's a generation younger than them. Now aged sixty, Arnon was born on the kibbutz, studied at the Bezalel Academy of Art and Design in Jerusalem, and worked as a cartoonist for *Al Ha'Mishmar*, the newspaper affiliated with Mapam (the labor kibbutz movement's political wing and one of the predecessors of today's Meretz Party). At a young age, he frequented Mapam's leading intellectual circles. He also experienced from up close the collapse of Israel's party-driven press, a process that made him doubt his ideology, or at least its viability as a business model. After his adventures in journalism, he came back to the kibbutz and eventually became the publisher of the regional council's newspaper. We meet in his small office, which is full of newspapers and cartoons. "The power of a newspaper is in its independence," he states, "and this is a paper that fearlessly criticizes the regional council's decisions, even though four pages in each issue are the council's."

Avni may have won the privatization battle, but it's not easy for him to talk about the process; there are still residual bad feelings. "At first I was fighting everyone on my own. It was hard for me to even sit in the dining hall. But I realized that if we didn't make this change, the kibbutz would turn into an old-age home. As the years passed I got to know many of the kibbutz movement's leaders, people who extolled physical labor and all sorts of ideals that made them happy, but they themselves were not on the kibbutz and were not working in the dairy farm or the fields, and their happiness did not extend to the little people who got up to work every morning."

"How was the battle waged on the kibbutz?"

"Those of us who were in our fifties at the time led the campaign against the old-timers and the very young members—after all, when you're twenty you always think socialism is exciting. There was slander, gossip, you name it. I even had terrible fights with my own parents, but in the end they acknowledged that they'd been aware of the weaknesses their whole lives, but had turned a blind eye. It's like a religious person who sees that God doesn't answer his prayers but can't stop praying. I kept insisting that we had to bring economists to weigh in, and when they came you could see how many things the kibbutz, as an entity, prefers not to know. For example, it prefers not to know that a particular business is failing, because the losses are just rolled over into a different business. I said to them: You've done great things, you couldn't have done it any other way, but either we change now or we'll cease to exist."

"Perhaps people like you, who earn a good living, wanted to keep more of their profits to themselves and have a better quality of life?"

"Your premise is mistaken: the big earners on the kibbutz were actually firmly opposed to the idea. This is a struggle over an idea. And it tore us apart."

Arnon stayed in Nirim during the war; he can't be bothered to travel all over Israel and inconvenience relatives and friends. Politically, like many of his peers, he has moderated his opinions in the past few years, moving more to the center. "We're not talking about peace anymore, it's impractical," he says. "Most of the people here vote Meretz or Labor, but now there are more doubts.

We have to accept the existence of the Palestinian nation, and we played a part in their tragedy. If you look at things with historical perspective, it's obvious that we can't control them forever. There are four million Palestinians between the Mediterranean and the Jordan River, who are going to become Israeli citizens. That is my greatest political nightmare. I have a recurrent dream: I'm standing with a gun at the gates of the kibbutz, and all the way to the horizon I see Arabs who've knocked down the fence and are running at me. I stand there shooting at them one by one, but there are so many of them, and they keep moving toward me."

A symbolic dream, to say the least. "Do your kids live here?"

"My daughters left the kibbutz long before the change. Their decision to leave allowed me to see the demographic gulf. But now we do manage to attract young people. You're here in the middle of the war and it's hard to see, but Nirim, partly due to privatization, is in very good shape."

"How do you see the future?"

"When Israel goes to war, I stand with my country. And this is a war of no choice. But in general, if up to now the government has played with our lives and Israelis kept believing that if we crushed the Palestinians they'd be quiet—we've now seen that that is not happening. This vision of 'crushing them to pieces' has itself been crushed in this war. And unfortunately there is nothing else."

The kibbutz dining hall no longer serves dinner, only lunch: one of privatization's outcomes. But the meals are impressively abundant. Perhaps because of my childhood memories of time spent on kibbutzim, I select two entrees, but someone whispers that I'll have to pay double. And then I see the check-out line, a feature that was never present in those childhood kibbutz visits. The dining hall is managed by Adi Lagziel, a young woman who makes a point of mentioning her Tripoli roots, perhaps in an ironic nod to the kibbutz's Ashkenazi dominance.

Adi is in her thirties, representing the fourth age-group we meet on Nirim. She grew up in Holon, a city on the south end of metropolitan Tel Aviv, and studied pastry-making, and she and her husband decided to set up their home in Nirim. They moved here in 2007 and have two children. She didn't always dream about a kibbutz or a collective life, but was looking for a place where her family could have the best possible life. In a month, after seven years on the kibbutz, their official absorption process as members is set to begin. That means they will purchase a plot on the kibbutz and invest all their savings in this place. Adi says this is probably the most difficult decision of her life. "The first time I got caught in a 'Red Color' warning, I felt like a mouse in a trap. To this day when I'm alone I react differently to the air-raid sirens. When I'm with the kids I smile and say, 'Who is going to bring the playing cards?' I've turned them from very independent kids into children who only play outside when I'm with them. Kids with restrictions." She is extremely anxious. She spent almost a month away from the kibbutz with her children, and if the ceasefire is not extended tonight at midnight, they will leave again. The bags are already packed. It's not yet clear if they'll go to her parents or find some other arrangement.

I ask why she would stay here and invest her capital in the kibbutz.

"I have a brother who lives abroad, and one day he wrote to me, 'This is not your home. Get up and leave.' But to go back to the city and have the kids shut up in an apartment—that's crazy to me. We were the first family who came here as non-member residents. I rent an apartment and I pay my bills. But I know this: there's nowhere else in Israel where I can get this quality of life. I couldn't find this kind of education for my kids anywhere else in the country, unless it's at prices I can't afford."

"So you'll end up staying here because of the kids?"

"Perhaps. Ultimately, this is the best life I can give them, despite everything." When she lived in the Tel Aviv area she always voted Likud, Adi says, "but everything changed when they shot at me."

"Why?"

"Because they shot at me and at my kids!"

"Where are you now, politically?"

"The Palestinians are not gentle people, but neither are we. There were days in the war when I said: if they just let Lieberman run the war, maybe all this will be resolved.[6] But that's just dreaming. I don't know what my opinions are. I live in the last row of housing on the kibbutz, and every day I see Gaza from my window. That's my political opinion."

---

6 Avigdor Lieberman, Israel's Minister of Defense and former Minister of Foreign Affairs, known for his right-wing views and belligerent statements.

* * *

At five o'clock in the afternoon, with seven hours to go before the ceasefire expires, the swimming pool is full of kids spraying each other with water rifles, floating on pool mattresses, a medley of colorful bathing suits quivering in the water. Many young couples on the lawn push strollers and rock baby-bouncers, infants wail, and on the far side a barbeque grill sends up flames and smoke. To my surprise, I learn that each family must bring their own meat to grill. "Privatization," a young woman explains disdainfully when I comment, and lounges back in her chair. One does hear complaints about privatization, but it seems clear that just as with capitalism—many of whose critics can't truly envision the new order that would arise on its ruins—most people on Nirim accept the transition with understanding and have adapted, albeit sometimes grumblingly, to the winds of change. They acknowledge that the kibbutz has made it through the transition successfully, that today the tables have turned and that, given the cost of living in Israel, life on a flourishing kibbutz has once again become desirable. People may not come to Nirim now for the ideological reasons that led Moshe Etzion here in the seventies, but one could say that the kibbutz's transformation over the past decade is parallel to one that Israel as a whole has experienced since the mid-1980s, after the plan to resuscitate the economy—overseen by Shimon Peres in 1985—led to diminished government intervention and to the privatization of state companies and social services.

The pool party is a summer celebration of sorts. Many of the members are reuniting after being away from the kibbutz. Rotem and Eynav sit on deckchairs wearing sunglasses, enjoying the warm breeze. Rotem asks for a cigarette and says she took up smoking again because of the war. "Our suitcases are still packed. I'm debating what to do if the ceasefire runs out at midnight." At first glance everything may look normal at this shindig, with blue skies and smiling people, kids shouting and playing, but a brief conversation with a local is enough to fracture the party's relaxed veneer.

Rotem's three kids are in the pool, as is Eynav's son. Rotem left the kibbutz for ten years and came back for her kids' sake. She says she always knew a kibbutz childhood was the best gift you could give a kid. But if the ceasefire doesn't hold she'll move away. "I'm depressed," says Eynav. She is contemplating leaving the kibbutz for good. "I've been here for four years. We left Tel Aviv both because of the kids and because it was so expensive there. I've been wandering around the country for weeks now, and I'm exhausted." Unlike Eynav, Rotem is a kibbutz member. In fact, she and her husband are the most recent couple to have been made members. So for them, leaving is not an option. Her husband voted against privatization. "Families like ours, with three kids, paid the highest price for privatization," she explains, "mostly because of the education costs, which suddenly soared. For people in their fifties or older, it didn't make that much of a difference, so they supported it."

"My husband used to be on the right, but now he's changed

his opinions," she continues. "I stayed pretty left-wing." She adds that new people have been coming to the kibbutz recently, from the Tel Aviv area, bringing different political opinions. Some of them even vote for Likud and Lieberman. Eynav says she doesn't feel like talking politics; she's troubled by the effects of the war on her son. "I've noticed that he's becoming a lot more militant, all of a sudden everything is guns and tanks and rifles. I find that very sad."

The sky is getting darker. It'll be evening soon. I hear a whisper in my ear.

"Have you asked yourself where the blacks are?"

I turn around but the young man is already walking away. I follow him. "Are you a kibbutz member?" I ask.

"I'm black, how could I be a kibbutz member?" he laughs. "I'm married to a kibbutz native." He doesn't want to give his name. He's lived on Nirim for a few years and they have kids. "My opinions may be on the left, but the reality here is right-wing. A majority of people on the left are deluded, they have to understand that our most educated people are trying to talk with people in Gaza from two hundred years ago. In the end, technology will beat out religion." I ask about his whispered overture. "I was joking a little," he says, trying to backtrack. "The best life in Israel today is on the kibbutzim, they have excellent education. People here are top quality, but it's a certain species, very different. At first I felt weird here, I wasn't part of them. But now there are Russians here, and more Mizrahis. So everything's a little less Ashkenazi."

I tell him I've heard about people who are considering leaving. After all, they've been shot at for a month now.

"Look at that," he says, pointing to the pool. "Just another day on the kibbutz, five in the afternoon, parents and kids in the pool together—where can you find that in the city? You think anyone's going to leave a life like this?"

Postscript

While on Nirim, I met the father and the son of Zeev Etzion, the kibbutz's military security co-ordinator, both of whom are mentioned in this chapter. I wanted to talk with Zeev himself, and we did meet briefly in the dining hall, but in the heat of events we did not find time for a proper conversation. Three weeks later, on the last day of Operation Protective Edge, Zeev Etzion and his friend Shahar Melamed were killed by a mortar shell.

I Feel Al-Aqsa in All My Body
East Jerusalem

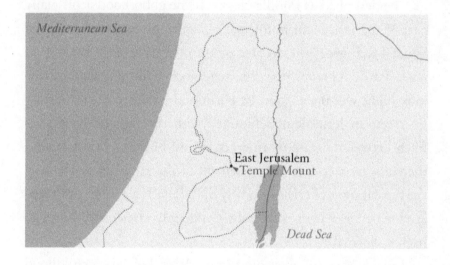

A police blockade has been erected at the turn-off from the Jerusalem–Ramallah road to Shuafat, a Palestinian neighborhood in northeast Jerusalem. A tractor clears debris off the partially burnt asphalt: glass shards, junk, scrap metal and concrete barriers. It's morning, and the streets are nearly deserted apart from several police vehicles. There are some shoppers in the bakery, the butcher's and the grocery store. Mohammed Abu

Khdeir, a sixteen-year-old resident of Shuafat, was murdered
this week. The murderers, local Jews, burned him alive. They
were out for revenge after Hamas operatives murdered the three
Jewish boys whose bodies were eventually found near Halhul, a
small town just north of Hebron. The murder of Abu Khdeir led
to unprecedented riots, and today the police are barring Jewish-
owned vehicles from entering Shuafat.

Some thirty-five thousand people live here, most of whom
may be described as middle-class. The neighborhood is officially
part of the Jerusalem municipality, not to be confused with the
Shuafat Refugee Camp located on the other side of the separation
wall. Two days from now, the roadblock will be gone and free
movement will once again be permitted in this part of the city.
Everyone in Jerusalem is familiar with the frenetic back-and-
forth between a state of emergency and business as usual, and
there always seems to be an element of the arbitrary in the way
the typical signs of crisis—mostly manifested in a more rigid separation between Jews and Arabs—suddenly vanish and things go
back to normal.

I think back to an evening in my West Jerusalem childhood
home in Beit Ha'Kerem. It must have been around 1989, and a
Jewish man had been stabbed in town earlier that day. A group of
us neighborhood kids gathered at the little commercial strip, and
some of them wanted to chase down Arabs in revenge—it didn't
matter where they were from, as long as they were Arabs. They
said their friends had caught two Arabs on the nearby main road
and "beat the crap out of them." A small group among us objected

to beating Arabs merely because one Arab had murdered a Jew, but most of the kids insisted we had no choice. Someone said something about an eye for an eye, and other more-or-less accurate biblical quotes were thrown out. The confrontation escalated into threats and shoves, but in the end we got tired and everyone went home. About two weeks later we played soccer with Arab boys in Sacher Park. Some of the kids who'd wanted to catch Arabs that night were there too.

"You don't talk about Jewish terrorism," a man at the butcher shop observes, "only Palestinian terrorism. I watch your TV channels every morning, and there's no such thing as Jewish terrorism."

On a wall alongside the main road at the bottom of a small hill, there is a giant poster of Mohammed Abu Khdeir. A large mourning tent has been set up opposite the picture. There are lots of chairs arranged in rows, but there aren't many people here yet. Two kids sit whispering and yawning, giving the mourners bored looks and edging toward the side of the tent. I sit down by a group of men in their fifties, and their anger at Israeli society bursts out quickly.

"You only broadcast what's convenient for you. We don't believe a word on Israeli media," someone says. His son drives a bus on the Jerusalem–Tel Aviv route, his daughter is studying education at the Open University; both live in the neighborhood. He doesn't want to give his name. "It doesn't matter anyway," he laughs, "your security services will recognize me by the data. I've got to the age of fifty-five, I've been through lots of events, and what have I seen? Mostly racism. Every year it gets worse."

"Most of the racism is from the Jewish side," a friend concurs, "not the Arab side. A little boy is kidnapped five minutes away from a mosque and burned alive—where are we? Is this Hitler's Germany? There are three Jewish kids whom you claim were kidnapped, they were found dead with no smell, no flies, no nothing—they had an accident on the way to Eilat." I ask the others if they really subscribe to that version of events. Indeed, most of them don't believe the boys were kidnapped by Hamas. A few conspiracy theories are offered, the most common one being that the boys were killed in an accident on their way to Eilat, which the security services then exploited for their own ends. I am taken aback by these outlandish scenarios, but I slowly understand that the lack of faith in all Israeli institutions—their intentions, their versions, their acts—infiltrates almost every word these men say.

They see a contradiction between the mantle of Israeli democracy and the preferential treatment of Jews by virtually all Israeli institutions. This discrimination is often portrayed in Israeli discourse as being either accidental, necessitated by circumstances, or soon-to-be-rectified, but the Palestinians view such justifications as a fiction that Jews like to tell themselves. Where Jewish Israelis perceive a complex incongruity between democracy and Jewish supremacy, these men see only a powerful machine whose every arm is dedicated to fulfilling Jewish aspirations, and they spend most of their lives lost in its labyrinthine parts. I've heard similar talk throughout the West Bank, but the residents of Shuafat are significantly closer to the center of life in West Jerusalem, and their contact with the authorities—namely, with Jews—is daily.

"As a father and a grandfather," Bassam, a semitrailer driver, tells me, "I'm afraid for my kids and my grandkids. I'm afraid that what happened to Mohammed will happen to them. Every father in East Jerusalem is afraid now. Maybe we can't live together anymore."

A teenager named Tariq Abu Khdeir walks past. He is Mohammed's cousin, a United States citizen who was brutally beaten by the Israeli Border Police yesterday. The incident was caught on camera and went viral all over the world. It happened a few days after Mohammed's murder. Tariq's face is bandaged and he has a black-and-blue shiner under one eye. He wears a gray shirt and jeans, and is telling an American journalist about the attack. A German reporter squeezes in and asks if he has anything to say to the police who beat him. "Think before you do something," Abu Khdeir replies in English, "the people here are not the problem, the state violence is." They ask if he'll come back, and he says he'll come to visit every year. More journalists gather around, shoving microphones and cameras in his face, and he dutifully answers all their questions.

Every so often a member of Knesset or some other public figure arrives in the tent. The cameramen and reporters hurry after them and document them giving speeches next to Mohammed's father. Most of the crowd observes these dignitaries with boredom and sometimes mockery; they've seen this show before. "There's the guy from Balad who's always going for drama," one of the men we met earlier whispers to me, and, on cue, the Knesset member from the largest Israeli-Arab party stands in the middle of the tent and delivers a long speech in Arabic.

I approach Mohammed's father and mumble something about how sorry I am. I know how meaningless my words sound, like everything he hears here probably does. He looks tired; his blue eyes are very bloodshot. "Think about him," one relative told me, "he stands here with all these people, talking politely, but his mind—what is it full of? Only one thing. He's picturing the final moments of his son, who sat in the car with them and was almost beaten to death and finally burned. How can he even see anything else?"

Suddenly Mohammed's father asks me, "Did you see the pictures? Did you see what they did to him?"

As I nod, I look into his eyes and know with certainty that there is nothing I can say now: it's just words. He hears so many words. Faced with such a devastating loss, faced with a father who must picture over and over again the final moments of his son who was burned alive—it seems impertinent to use words.

Haneen Zoabi, a Palestinian-Israeli Knesset member from Balad, sits down near some other dignitaries. When someone shows her a poster advocating "Death Sentence for Haneen Zoabi," she laughs. Everyone seems to be expressing this fear now, not in its political sense but in a completely personal way, each applying it to their own family and children. Kids have been killed here in riots before, so the experience of mourning a child is not unfamiliar, but something in the viciousness of Mohammed Abu Khdeir's murder provokes deeper fears.

Across the street from the men's mourning tent, outside a private house, the women's tent has been erected. I go closer to the tent and stand outside, and a few women ask if I need anything. When they realize I'm Israeli, most of them go back to their own affairs. But Abira Abu Khdeir comes out to talk. And while the men in the tent used cautious tones and most asked not to be identified by name, Abira is fearless and gets right to the political heart of the matter. "All of Palestine is Palestine, from sea to sea. I don't believe there is such a thing as Israel. All the Israelis came here from far away and conquered our lands. If the Jews want to live in Palestine, go ahead, but give up on Israel. I don't believe in two states, it's just talk."

She speaks fast and furious, sometimes using terms or names I don't know, part of the neighborhood vernacular. She tells me her husband is in prison, and both her son and daughter have been imprisoned at various times. She is well acquainted with the Israeli security forces, who've come to see her more than once and asked her to act as their informant. "The man from Shin Bet came to my home one morning and said, 'We heard you threw a stone.' Then he asked, 'Where is your husband?' I told him, 'You know exactly where my husband is and you know I've never thrown so much as a button my whole life.' And he says to me, 'You know about everything that happens in Shuafat. I want us to talk on the phone every couple of days.' Then he gave a date when he'd come to see me again. You understand how your people work here?"

The Israeli press was up in arms recently, when the Shuafat

light rail station was burned down. They held the incident up as conclusive evidence of Jerusalem Palestinians' ungratefulness toward the municipality that brought progress to Shuafat. Abira Abu Khdeir is of a different opinion: the arson was not motivated by simple anger in the heat of the moment. She thinks people in Shuafat don't want the train here.

"A few years ago they came here with this train, and now every day Jews and settlers go through our neighborhood. That's why they burned the station down, they don't want the train, it's the reason our children are in danger. That train is not for us, we have our own transportation. Now the settlers are walking around here, shopping, cursing at us, a while ago they pulled a woman's hijab off. The train is for the settlers who live on the Shuafat Ridge." She walks me to the empty yard behind the mourners' tent, which serves as a smoking spot, and shows me the Jews' houses. She tells me that next to her house they built a road for the settlers. "We're all starting to think about it now. How will our children be okay? The Jews bring a train here for themselves and we keep quiet, and now they're burning our kids alive? In the building where I live there are fifteen children. I don't let my kids go out now."

I go back to the men's tent. My eye is caught by three kids sitting next to a colorful curtain, looking bored. They see me holding an unlit cigarette—smoking is forbidden because it's Ramadan—and motion toward the field beyond the curtain, where people go to smoke secretly. They giggle. I sit down next to them. One of them is Taha Abu Khdeir, a cousin of Mohammed, and the others are his friends Mustafa and Suliman. They're eighteen and work in an electrical lab. We converse in a mixture of Hebrew, English and Arabic. I tell them that my grandparents (from Syria, Yemen and Egypt) spoke fluent Arabic, but I'm just learning it now. Every so often they type something in Arabic on their iPhones and translate it into Hebrew with Google Translate to show me. When we discuss the Jewish murderers, they type out their demand "that their houses be demolished like they do to Palestinian murderers." I hear this equation frequently in the tent. The kids have probably spoken to journalists and have a fair understanding of the talking points. We speak about Mohammed, whom they say they were supposed to meet on the night he was snatched. I ask them to tell me about him, and they say he was "ambitious and kind and liked to laugh a lot." They ask where I work. I'm a writer, I explain. They demand evidence, and the four of us hunch over an iPhone while I show them newspaper articles. I tell them I met mothers here in Shuafat who are afraid their children will get hurt. When I ask if they're afraid, they answer just as adolescents should: "We're not scared of anything."

* * *

On a bright but cold winter day in Jerusalem, everything looks calm. Yesterday Ibrahim al-Akari, a married father of five from the Shuafat Refugee Camp, plowed his van into a crowd at the light rail station on Shimon Ha'Tzadik Street in East Jerusalem, intending to run over Jews. Superintendent Jadan Assad, a Border

Police officer from the Druze village of Beit Jann, was killed, and several people were injured. Al-Akari was shot dead. On his Facebook page he had posted items about the al-Aqsa Mosque (Islam's third holiest site, located in the Old City of Jerusalem) and about Yehuda Glick, an American-born rabbi who advocates for greater Jewish access to the Temple Mount, and who had just days earlier survived an assassination attempt. Al-Akari was clearly upset over recent fears about al-Aqsa, and he wasn't the only one. Over the past year many people have raised red flags about the simmering violence in Jerusalem, and since the murder of Mohammed Abu Khdeir in the summer and the subsequent riots it has bubbled over. "There is a quiet civil war raging in Jerusalem," a veteran city resident told me.

A long line of people wait outside Mughrabi Gate (also called Gate of the Moors), which since 1967 has been the only entrance to the Temple Mount accessible to non-Muslims, and a frequent point of contention. Most of the people here are international tourists, predominantly from Europe, though there is also a group of young women from Shanghai. The visitors are all excited and do not seem afraid, even though there was unrest here yesterday. The eastern entrance to the Western Wall is large and wide open, with visitors flowing in freely. Roughly a quarter of its width, and accessible only by a wooden bridge, Mughrabi Gate allows a slow trickle of visitors through. A glorious building with large windows looms over us. It serves as the worldwide center of Aish HaTorah, a flourishing ultra-Orthodox Jewish organization with an extensive outreach operation. "Come study with us and

discover the profound ideas that changed the world," the organization's website bids visitors. "Aish HaTorah invites every Jew
to come and rekindle the torch of Jewish awareness and pride.
In doing so, it contributes to the quelling of brotherly hatred in
Israel, and to the prevention of assimilation in the Diaspora."

After squeezing through the gate, visitors arrive at a hut
where they and their intentions are scrutinized. The tourists
march toward the Temple Mount, while three boys with yarmulkes sit on the bench waiting. For them, or more plainly, for
religious Jews, there is a separate procedure. The policeman on
duty asks their teacher, a young man with a beard and a grin,
"Anything special, or the usual round?" The man replies, "The
usual round." The boys, twelfth graders from a high school
yeshiva in Kiryat Arba, a Jewish settlement adjacent to Hebron,
giggle as we cross the wooden bridge and approach the mosque.
"Are you excited?" I ask them. "Yes! It's our first visit to the holy
temple." At the end of the bridge, just before the mosque plaza,
we run into dozens of policemen in full riot gear, with helmets
and guns, and the playful mood abruptly dissipates.

The square in front of the mosque is fairly empty, except for
two groups of Muslims sitting in circles. When we walk past
them, our police escorts remind us not to linger. I ask the Arabs
what they're discussing, and the policeman instructs me not to
talk to them. As the boys and their teacher walk past, one of the
Arab men shouts at the teacher, "Don't lie to them! You people
have nothing here!" The atmosphere on the Mount is not as tense
as it sometimes is, but it is gloomy, full of toxic suspicion. There

are procedures in place to separate Arabs from Jews, which every-one follows carefully—from the Israeli police to the men in suits and sunglasses who represent the Jerusalem Islamic Waqf. The Waqf has the authority to oversee the Temple Mount, decide when to open the gates—with the exception of Mughrabi Gate— and determine the rules of conduct on the Mount. Any deviation from the routine, even a few steps in the wrong direction, prompts whispers and quick responses. Everyone here acknowledges the volatility of the site and recognizes that a firm hand is needed to prevent the apocalypse of a religious war breaking out at the Temple Mount, a scenario reporters around the world are fond of exploring.

Someone in the Palestinian group next to us says, "We're not al-Mourabitoun or anything like that, we're just here to pray. Everything comes from Allah." Al-Mourabitoun is a group of young Palestinian men and women, from Jerusalem and else-where, who monitor the Temple Mount and send out warnings whenever Jews ascend, especially religious Jews. It is an unarmed patrol of sorts, meant to protect Islamic holy sites against Jewish plots. Lately, and unrelated to the murder carried out yesterday by Ibrahim al-Akari, more and more Palestinians have been fear-ful of the fate of al-Aqsa, and these are not only devout Muslims. The Israeli government accuses the Palestinian Authority and Hamas of fanning the flames around the Temple Mount, and perhaps that is also true, but it seems that the profound concern voiced by Palestinians on the street is more than simply the out-come of propaganda, and stems mostly from their suspicion of anything the Jewish establishment does in Jerusalem. It's not only Jewish visitors to the Temple Mount, but activities carried out by Jewish institutions—which consistently strive to take over more and more land, houses and assets for Jewish use—that make Palestinians in Jerusalem believe that "the Jews are plotting something at al-Aqsa."

Their suspicions are not unfounded, as an examination of the data makes clear. East Jerusalem has just over three hundred thousand Palestinian residents. According to 2012 data, seventy-seven percent of them live under the poverty line, including 119,000 children.

I listen to the teacher from Kiryat Arba explain to his students how the incline next to us was created: "King Solomon wanted to enable many visitors to come here. Unlike the Muslims, who don't want members of other religions here, God says, 'My house shall be called a house of prayer for all peoples.'" The boys listen intently. "The Jewish tradition tells us that here the world was created, here is the apex of the place! There is a huge connection between something earthly and something spiritual."

I remind the teacher that, for many years, rabbis from all streams of Judaism forbade Jews from coming up to the Temple Mount. The prohibition was accepted by most adjudicators before 1967, and even afterwards there was consent among the Chief Rabbinate, the ultra-Orthodox rabbis and the Zionist-nationalist rabbis: Jews were not supposed to visit the Temple Mount "as per the rules of the Torah," and because of its sanctity. I ask why he thinks this has changed in the past few years.

"The Council of Rabbis of Judea and Samaria determined in the nineties that the ascent is permitted, and called on all rabbis themselves to ascend and to guide their communities to do so," he replies. "And today there are several rabbis in religious Zionism who permit the ascent to the Temple Mount, as they assume we will know how to ascend in purity and not desecrate the Holy Temple."

The boys, ordinary adolescents with all the requisite mannerisms, including a certain shyness that vanishes in an instant, listen with interest. They admit they had trouble sleeping because they were so excited. "It's scary," they say, "but we've known for a long time that we'd come here in our last year of high school." I ask how they feel about touring this place with an armed police guard. The teacher concedes he feels uncomfortable, and he understands the Muslim worshippers' difficulty, "But this place does not belong only to them or only to the Jews, it belongs to the whole world. In the past, Gentiles were not allowed to approach the wall of the Temple Mount, but the minute the Temple was built Solomon wanted to give them the opportunity to pray, so he expanded the Mount. We must live with the fact that there are people who have trouble with our presence here, but the People of Israel must be connected with this place." He gives me a perplexed look: "Don't you feel anything?"

One of the police officers says there was "a lot of thinning-out" today, and they gave permits only to Muslims over the age of forty to come to the Mount. A minute later he adds that they've actually done that for the past several weeks. Meanwhile, the teacher points to the mosque's arches and says this is where the Temple's daily activities were conducted. A few people in their early twenties join us, quietly observing the platform with glazed eyes. One of them appears to be weeping. Are you crying from emotion? I ask. "I'm crying because I don't feel anything," he admits.

One of the newcomers is a relative of Yehuda Glick, but he asks me not to give his name. He used to live in Gush Katif, the Jewish settlement bloc in Gaza that was evacuated by the Israeli government in 2005, and is now at King David Yeshiva on Mount Zion in Jerusalem. The day starts early for the yeshiva students, all in their twenties, and in addition to their religious studies they play music, discuss philosophy and hike around Jerusalem a lot. "I really enjoy it. The place is hypnotizing. I can really feel the holiness." He knows a lot about the history of the Temple Mount, and talks about radiocarbon dating tests conducted by universities, which found that a few of the beams did originate in the First Temple and Second Temple periods. Afterwards, he says, the Arabs sold the beams. "What part of the Holy Temple were we supposed to see now?" he asks his friends. "The northern interior," he answers for them. "Our sages say the sanctity of the site can awaken the heart. We have an opportunity here to direct our hearts to the Lord."

We stand facing the steps that lead to the Dome of the Rock. The young Jews stop at the bottom of the steps as the Arabs look down from the top, while the Jewish police and Waqf officials position themselves along the middle, forming a barrier between the two groups. There is tension between the Israeli police and the Waqf, too, and they barely speak. Sometimes the Waqf men protest the influx of Jewish visitors, and sometimes Israeli officers flag an Arab presence they deem insubordinate.

The Waqf officials are displeased with the young Jews' proximity to the Dome of the Rock. The Jews ask to stay for another moment. Now the Waqf officials suspect the young men are actually murmuring prayers, which is against the rules. The decision to prohibit Jews from praying on the Temple Mount was reached after the '67 war by an Israeli ministerial committee established to protect religious sites. The young men from the yeshiva told us, "That is exactly what Yehuda Glick was fighting against." But how can one tell if these young people are in fact silently praying? The Waqf officials urge the police to take care of the youngsters, and the latter hurry the visitors along, but by now the Arabs at the top of the steps are visibly agitated and they can be heard tossing the occasional provocation at the Jews. Everyone scrutinizes everyone else, looking for the slightest misstep. There can be no impulsive moves here. "We get along with the police," a Waqf man tells me. "Sometimes there are issues, but we get along."

We leave the square and head to the Temple Mount exit. A policeman tells me that, as long as we were inside, we were in a sterile zone controlled by the police, but outside, in the Old City, arrangements are more murky: people roam freely, and trouble frequently erupts. Out there, we will also encounter al-Mourabitaat, the women's division of the informal Temple Mount guard. "Get ready for a ruckus," the policeman whispers. Just before the exit gate, the Waqf man points out a handsome stone building with its curtains drawn. "Four Arab families live there, about two hundred feet from the Dome of the Rock." Someone asks how much an apartment costs. "Millions," he laughs, "much more expensive than Tel Aviv. These are the closest apartments to the Dome of the Rock, and they'll never build anything closer."

As soon as we leave the Temple Mount and start walking the alleyways of the Old City, we hear whistles and loud shouts of *"Allahu akbar!"* Perhaps because we can't see anything and the voices echo over us, it sounds like a major commotion. But from up close we see only a police barrier manned by two tired policewomen, with about twenty Palestinian women crowding behind them: al-Mourabitaat. I notice that the teacher and his students are gone, having slipped away near the Netiv Aryeh Yeshiva building to make their way to the Western Wall. One of the young men from Glick's group calls me over, and I join him next to the yeshiva's front door, which is hidden from the view of al-Mourabitaat. I am hoping he has something interesting to add, but he just asks me not to mention his name. It's a familiar request, from both Palestinians and Jews. The entire Jewish group vanishes then, and we're left to face the Palestinian women's derogatory calls alone.

"Why does it bother you that Jews come here?" I ask them.

"Al-Aqsa is ours," one woman answers. Their shouts suddenly grow louder—the atmosphere ignites every time a religious-looking Jew walks past, which happens frequently, given the proximity of Netiv Aryeh Yeshiva. Sometimes the women lean against the yeshiva's wall, tired from their long shifts. When religious Jews are not around, these women are courteous, although they are understandably suspicious of the intents of any Jew hanging around al-Aqsa. "We can't live with you," another woman tells me, "we want our own state. The Jews can go back to America or Europe." A young man wearing designer jeans, a fashionable scarf and black patent leather shoes, says, "I saw how your people burned the boy from Shuafat. The day will come when all the Jews will come here to the Temple Mount, and they'll all get their heads cut off." A native of Jerusalem who works in the city, he does not seem to intend to provoke—his statement is more of a comment on Jews in general and the reckoning that surely must happen eventually. "We're prepared to die for al-Aqsa. I feel al-Aqsa in all my body. I want to live quietly and I've always wanted peace, but the Jews in Jerusalem keep aggravating us. And now we say: if you come near al-Aqsa, you're done for. The entire Arab world will come here to get rid of you." We speak in English and occasionally Arabic, which someone translates for me. No one here would talk Hebrew.

A young ultra-Orthodox man who happens by is showered with curses. He gives the women a big grin, puts his fingers to his lips provocatively, then makes a "bring it on!" gesture. The policewomen hurry him away. Dozens of such hostilities between Jews and Arabs occur here every day, little non-violent confrontations—curses, insults, mockery—that often reach childish levels of pettiness, with one woman brandishing the Koran and another man waving his Tanach. The Jews know the police will always protect them. "It's true, they're not afraid," admits one of the Palestinians, a young woman in her twenties who's here on her day off from university studies. "Understand this: we have no hatred toward the Jews. You created this hatred by allowing your Jews access to al-Aqsa, and they curse Muhammad. Why don't you punish them? Why aren't I allowed to walk around the Western Wall like you're allowed to walk around al-Aqsa? There will never be peace, God knows." Her grandfather used to live in Lod, and she says he often told her, "We were neighbors, Jews and Arabs, and we had good relations. But nowadays Jews and Arabs don't even say hello to each other." Oddly enough, there is not much ferment here today, but more of a familiar ritual that everyone wearily follows. Yesterday tensions were high, the women report, and there were gas grenades thrown and the police beat them.

One of the Palestinian guard women is about fifty, and her fluent English is inflected with a slight American accent. She is taller than the other women and speaks freely with both Jews and Arabs, but she will not reveal her name. Unlike most of the women here, she is familiar with the liberal discourse of human rights, and puts it to good use. Her husband's family is from Jerusalem, but she was born and raised in New Jersey. One day her husband decided to move the family to Jerusalem, and she went along with the plan but without much enthusiasm. "I knew it would be difficult, but I didn't expect it to be this difficult. The run-ins between Jews and Arabs frighten me, there is deep racism toward Arabs here, the Palestinians have virtually no rights and the Jews have all the rights. There is constant pressure for Jewish expansion here, they're always pushing the Palestinians out of Jerusalem. In the United States there are courts for these kinds of affairs, in Jerusalem there's nothing. At first I was naive and I told my friends, 'Let's go to the municipality, to the courts, to the press,' but I gradually learned that those institutions serve the Jews' needs. And it's completely transparent, it's out on the table, they don't hide it like they do in other places in the world. Did they demolish the houses of the Jews who murdered Mohammed Abu Khdeir? There's no point in exposing the discrimination over and over again, everyone knows all about it. Here: I want to pray at al-Aqsa now, but I can't."

"How do you see the future?"

"There are two ethnic groups here who have to get along. The Palestinians need their rights, rights that every ethnic group in the world deserves. We can't build here, we can't determine our own fate, on every street corner a Jewish representative with a court order awaits us. I want my country back, the holy sites back. We want freedom, without checkpoints, without violence, without police tearing our head-scarves off. It's hard for me to believe in co-existence with Jews, because every day I learn all over again how impossible it is."

I ask about her relocation to Jerusalem, the transition from being an American citizen with equal rights, at least on the surface, to being a Palestinian in Jerusalem. Is this where she wants to raise her children?

"Yes," she replies. "I want my children to live here. They'll learn religion, they'll learn their nationality. But after that, it's up to them. My older son couldn't get into the Hebrew University so he's studying architecture in Germany. He's at the top of his class."

It turns out not everyone in her family is here. Her older children have left Jerusalem to pursue different things. So the son is in Germany, two daughters are back in the US, and her three younger kids live here. "Everyone asks me: How come you don't go back to New Jersey? Not only Jews, I mainly hear it from Palestinians. I tell them I do miss it there, but I won't go back. When my husband wanted to move to Jerusalem I was against it, I was born in the US and I had a pretty good life there. The first year here was terrible. I was stunned by my status as a Palestinian. I had heard and read about it, but it's different to live it every day, to face the Jewish establishment, the police, to learn all the prohibitions. But I've been here for eighteen years and I don't regret it. When I stand here protecting al-Aqsa, I realize this is my place."

I say goodbye to al-Mourabitaat. When you get some distance from the Temple Mount and wander around the picture-perfect alleys of the Old City on a sunny spring day, the atmosphere changes. You could almost imagine you were in the ancient and slightly gentrified district of any European city, strolling among old buildings, souvenir stores, restaurants and other tourist traps, surrounded by crowds of joyous pilgrims. Among the colors I spot are a Ghanaian flag, hats that say "Bahrain 2000," shirts emblazoned with India's orange, white and green, and two kites with Portugal's colors. A medley of languages rings out from every corner, English and Spanish and Portuguese and Chinese. Children run around shouting, people pose for cameras. Every so often I run into one of the al-Mourabitaat women who were swearing in al-Aqsa's name outside the Temple Mount, now blending into the noisy, cheerful crowds vying to snap pictures of a Muslim man kneeling in prayer in a room that faces the Via Dolorosa.

On the way down to Lions Gate, I push my way between a guide carrying a Swedish flag and a few stragglers trailing a group from Bahrain, and I reach the Gate of the Tribes, which leads to al-Aqsa. Now the Mount is full of Muslim worshippers. "This gate is only for Muslims," says the policeman, "no Jews allowed." A man in a black overall stops next to me. "All Muslims are al-Mourabitoun," he offers. "It's very simple: we don't want Jews at al-Aqsa."

6

Do You Want to Be a King or a Prophet?

Kedumim and Elon Moreh

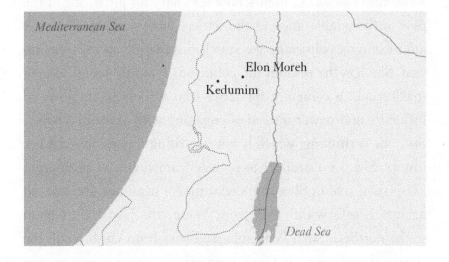

It's cold in Sarah Eliash's house. When I ask if she can turn the heat on, she laughs. The house is at the end of a small street in the settlement of Kedumim, about ten miles west of Nablus. From the living room window there is a view of olive trees along the Shomron mountains. Sarah's husband sits in the kitchen reading a book while she anxiously darts around the house. The phone rings off the hook. This is no ordinary day for the Eliashes: in a few hours, Sarah will go to Jerusalem to meet with Naftali Bennett, and later today she will officially declare her candidacy in the primaries for his party, Ha'Bayit Ha'Yehudi, ahead of the 2015 elections. I ask why her husband is reading instead of helping her; with just over a month until voting day, there's no time to waste. She says he's not enthusiastic about politics. Does she have a good chance of being elected? Yes, she says.

I came here to meet the legendary founder and principal of Kedumim's *ulpana* (a high-school seminary for girls), one of the most influential women in the settlers movement, but in fact I am meeting a politician. She scowls distastefully at my observation. She has the disdain for politicians typically found among intellectuals, a contempt for those who wallow in the mire of influence and power instead of engaging with existential issues. Still, she is running, which is not surprising if one considers her history. She is no stranger to political campaigns: in addition to her pivotal role in Shomron's educational institutes, she lobbied against Israel's withdrawal from Yamit, the Jewish settlement in the northern Sinai Peninsula, and later from Gush Katif, the cluster of settlements in Gaza, even going so far as to relocate her home to both places. After the 2005 evacuation of Gush Katif, known as "the disengagement," and her profound disappointment in the Yesha Council, which she believes did not oppose the government forcefully enough, Eliash spearheaded a reorganization of the council and served as the new deputy chair under Dani Dayan, whom we met earlier.

"I invested untold hours in that," she recounts. "After the

expulsion from Gush Katif, we realized that the heads of the Yesha Council had a lot of goals and budgets, and that they had systemic reasons for giving in to the regime. And then we set up the new council, as a lesson learned from the disengagement."

"Then why the Knesset?"

"I see it as a mission. But I do wonder if I will be able to have an influence. I hate to waste ninety percent of my time on politics."

It seems rather redundant to lament the politicking in politics, I point out, as opposed to, say, in academia or cultural institutions or a bank. It's just that the political system has its own rituals of elections and public struggles for power. In fact, unlike other systems—academia, for example—in which promotions might rely mostly on internal politics and the ability to flatter one's benefactors, in politics one usually has to go to the public and ask for its support. Ha'Bayit Ha'Yehudi is doing well in the polls, and I hardly meet a settler who isn't running for the Knesset. I ask Eliash about Bennett's vision of transforming his movement from a settlers' party to an all-Israeli party. Given her ideological standpoint, is she not worried that the party will end up like a smorgasbord of brittle positions?

"I identify strongly with Bennett's all-Israeli direction. The trend toward splitting up—these divisions into many subtle distinctions—is extremely damaging. We must invest in a search for the things that connect us. Our sector aspires to leadership positions. It was a subdued aspiration, ashamed even, which emerged after the 1967 war and came to fruition in the past decade. You can't lead from the margins. Sometimes I ask people: Do you want to be a king or a prophet? We are looking for monarchy now."

Sarah Eliash was born in the United States and came to Israel at the age of six months. She grew up on a religious moshav in the north of Israel. Her father was a Holocaust survivor who had escaped the Death March. After the war he was offered Swiss citizenship but declined, saying the only place he would move to was Israel. Eliash grew up with "a strong Zionist consciousness" and a religious education. In the sixties she studied physics at the Hebrew University in Jerusalem and later earned a master's degree in philosophy of science from Tel Aviv University. She married and moved to Ganei Tikva, a well-to-do Tel Aviv suburb. And then the '67 war broke out, leading to the growth of Gush Emunim, a movement that—unlike secular Zionism, which believed it had achieved its aims in the '67 war and came to a standstill—sketched out a clear vision for the future. Kedumim, founded in 1975, was the first community built in the Shomron after the war, and Eliash, who came here thirty-eight years ago, was a founding member. She says the first years here were euphoric. When people asked her back then why she chose to live in a trailer without running water or power, she said that it was on these paths that our biblical forefathers, Abraham, Yitzhak and Yaakov, had walked.

I remark that she sounds nostalgic for that era, although it's only in recent years that the settlement movement's victory has really been cemented.

She quotes Shulamit Aloni, a long-time Knesset member and leader of the left-wing party Meretz, who said, after the '67 war, "The vision of generations has come true." Eliash mentions other public figures identified with the secular left—or at least with secularism—including poets Nathan Alterman and Haim Gouri. She remembers the widespread euphoria after the war, and a recognition on the part of the vast majority of Jews that the land must be settled. Yes, she is nostalgic, because for her it was a time when secular and religious Zionism united for a religious and political moment, some might say a messianic moment, in which they shared a similar vision of the future. It was a moment whose loss still saddens her, and in some ways she still feels betrayed. It's as though everyone said, "Let's go!" but within a few years the settlers were left on their own, and ultimately became the secularists' enemies. All of a sudden she and her cohort were "a cancer in the state's body," she laments, quoting an oft-repeated diagnosis attributed to various left and center-left sources.

"As a child," Eliash continues, "I read books about the Etzel and the Palmach, the generation that established the state, and the first immigrants, and I always regretted not having been born in that time.[7] The first waves of immigration were an era of biblical proportions." She recalls relating powerfully to the ideas of Abraham Isaac Kook, the first chief rabbi of pre-State Israel and

---

7 The Etzel and the Palmach were paramilitary organizations that spearheaded Jewish resistance to the British Mandate in Palestine before the establishment of the State of Israel.

a renowned religious scholar and Jewish philosopher. "He had a very optimistic outlook. In the introduction to his book *The Lights of Penitence* he writes: 'Every generation shines with its own quality.' Meaning, each generation has a quality, something great that must be done, and we saw that in the settlement movement. I accept the historiosophical approach that sees a broader Jewish pattern of diaspora and revival, in which, through our presence here, we are now in the heart of a process of redemption. Our acts must be seen in that light."

Eliash is amused by the way secular Israelis denigrate the settlers as "messianic" without truly understanding what the term means. She says she certainly does live with a messianic consciousness—not of a personal Messiah, but an awareness that the messianic presence is embedded in every act, in nature itself, in the emergent reality of a free nation in its own land. She mentions the historian Jacob Talmon, and we discuss secular messianism according to Talmon's and others' definition of totalitarian ideologies (such as Nazism and Communism) that are based on an essential movement toward personal and political redemption and an essential change in world order. She has also read Hegel, as well as other philosophers, and has absorbed the sophisticated historical and dialectical view that motion does not always proceed in one direction, but may occur in many different directions, with each event redefining the others. When asked about Israel's so-called "hilltop youth," the population of young, mostly religious, radically nationalist settlers who work to establish illegal outposts throughout the West Bank, Eliash invokes the image of their post-'67 predecessors: "They're acting out their enthusiasm for revival. They do not simply want to preserve the accomplishments of the older generation."

"Because preservation means lack of motion?"

"Exactly. They're not interested in preserving the old, but in creating something of their own. Man seeks to be part of something larger."

"Could we refine that idea?"

"I live with a constant sense of miracle and wonder. Sometimes I step out of the minor events of today or yesterday and I realize that Jews have dreamed of this for two thousand years, and now here I am. There is a verse in Proverbs: 'Who shall ascend into the mountain of the Lord? And who shall stand in His holy place?' To ascend with great enthusiasm might be easy. To stay is the meaningful thing. The Sisyphean thing."

"So you stayed, and you appear to have won. The West Bank is full of settlements, all of Israeli society is implicated in the enterprise by now. But you are still disappointed in those who do not see the light. Here in the settlements, the shadow of the left wing looms so large it's as if we were still in the 1970s. Why does the losing camp's opinion matter so much?"

"Because it's a controversial victory," Eliash explains. "Something in me is always searching for harmony. I have a very difficult time with conflict. Perhaps that is why I have devoted years to finding the element that can unify religious and secular people. I really don't understand how the left wing hasn't experienced anything comparable to what we experience here. To me, the State of Israel is an accomplishment. The settlement here following the Six-Day War restored a sense of heroism."

"Criticism is leveled throughout the Jewish world at the settlement movement for having reduced complex and often multifaceted ideas into a land fetish. Do you identify with at least some of that criticism?"

"Despite the common view among the left, there is always conflict in our camp too. I read a lot of works by Rabbi Léon Ashkenazi, a contemporary of the French-Jewish philosopher Emmanuel Levinas. And he says that the world stands on three things, right? Torah, work and charity. Meaning, the world does not stand on one thing, and you are constantly moving between the poles, and that is the natural state, to have tension between contradictory positions. Lots of people here believe in one thing, and simplification helps them settle the contradictions. But public figures like Benny Katzover or Moshe Levinger are extremely complex people.[8] The criticism leveled at us for being interested only in settling all the Land of Israel is untrue; there has been, for example, high social mobility here. There are Sephardis here, Ethiopians, Russians..."

"Every time I meet settlers they mention the social mobility, the settlements as a place for all Jewish society, where its diverse communities can mingle. It strikes me as a well-worn line of defense that seeks to argue that this is everyone's home, not only the Ashkenazi settlers."

---

8 Longtime outspoken leaders of the settler movement.

"Well, then I'll answer you from the opposite direction," Eliash responds. "If you look closely, you will find that many people of my generation live in development towns now, they're not in Judea and Samaria at all. We had a broader worldview, but it's true that the settlements are at its center."

"You integrate universal concepts of morality in your positions," I point out. "Talking with you, I don't hear only about Jews all the time. How do you align this perspective with the huge discrepancy between Jews' and Palestinians' rights where you live? A discrepancy that can be seen at every checkpoint, every courthouse, road, government office? What story must a person tell herself to believe that this is a reasonable state of affairs?"

"I'll tell you something that is not politically correct. I don't believe there is such a thing as a Palestinian nation. I think we made it up. Their distinctness in the Arab world does not justify another state. The Jews are a nation, that is clear, and they have a historic continuity and so they require a state. I do feel the need for moral justification for my life here, I want to act morally, I'm here with all of my Jewish history. But as for the Palestinians, Jordan's population is sixty percent Palestinian, so what is Jordan anyway? If you need a territorial solution, then there's Jordan."

"I don't want to be impolite," I explain, "but that argument is somewhat absurd. After all, you know that nations are flexible entities, often composed of myths and legends and a history that retroactively paves the very path that prophesied their own emergence. And now you want to convince the Palestinians that they're not a nation because they weren't a nation one hundred years ago? Who's next, the Italians?"

"With everything that's occurring now, like the Arab-Sunni Spring, the Arabs' nationalist awareness is very dubious. Today the safest place for Arabs in the Middle East is here. Even under occupation, their lives are freer and more democratic than in the Arab world." Eliash is growing exasperated. She leans back and looks to either side, then says she's glad she's amusing me. Tensions in the room are escalating. I explain that I was only referring to that one argument, but she seems generally suspicious of me. "My husband told me: Why do you even need this meeting? Nothing good will come of it."

"You never know," I say. "But back to our subject: here on the West Bank, how do you contend with the absolute Jewish supremacy, which is partially enforced militarily, controlling the lives of people who can't even vote for the entity that rules over them?"

"On a human level, seeing Arabs at the checkpoint is a side effect of a situation that I dislike. But let me be clear: I don't lose sleep over it. I think Arab society has so far failed to establish any democratic space—the democratic concept doesn't apply to them anywhere anyway. If we leave the territories do you think they'll be better off or worse off? I remember that when we left Nablus, they were cutting off people's hands and feet there. It is crystal clear to me that if we end the regime that you call the occupation and leave the territories, we would be hurting many innocent Palestinians."

"So you think the Palestinians who want the occupation to end are simply not seeing the light?"

"Your words come from an anti-colonialist attitude," she answers. "That is why the Europeans are against us, too, because our circumstances apparently remind them of their own history. But our regime here is much more enlightened."

"What future do you see? Do you agree with the idea of preserving the status quo, which has worked well until now? Or with Naftali Bennett's partial annexation? Or a single state?"

"We must not withdraw from Judea and Samaria. Our rights here and in the 1948 territories are exactly the same: if we have no place in Judea and Samaria, then we have no place in Tel Aviv. Uri Elitzur's one-state idea doesn't frighten me, although I do not support it at this time."

"What rights do Palestinians have in this arena?"

"We need to gradually give the Palestinians in the territories human rights, freedom of movement, rights within the Israeli justice system, and we must also give citizenship to those Palestinians who want it and who demonstrate loyalty to the State of Israel. At the same time we must help Palestinians emigrate from here with dignity. It's not a simple thing. I'm not proposing a binational state, we will not be able to give citizenship to everyone."

"In your view, after we naturalize some of the Palestinians and encourage others to emigrate, what sort of political entity will exist here?"

"Perhaps a Jewish state with a large Arab minority. Say, forty percent. We cannot maintain generations of Palestinians where the economic divide between them and their neighbors is so huge. Awarding citizenship to some of the Palestinians would change their economic status and their expectations for the future, and they would also be forced to change things about their behavior, like their textbooks, for example, which incite against Jews. If that scenario scares middle-class Jews living in central Israel, they shouldn't vote for me."

Driving to the seminary through Kedumim's well-manicured streets, I observe the scenery around Nablus, and again it seems we are surrounded by a pastoral landscape of olive trees and nothing more. In the seminary's courtyard, a few girls play with their cell phones, music blaring. Two of them wear fairly short skirts. Sarah Eliash stops to look them up and down. "Do you know how many arguments I've had over this issue of dress? How many hours I've devoted to meetings and debates with the students and their parents?" She has ten children of her own, and started running the seminary in 1982, after her second son was born. This institution is her life's work, and today it has more than a thousand students.

"What changes have you seen among the students over the years?"

"Unequivocally, their attitude toward their bodies," she asserts. "In my generation they told us we must be modest and even hide our bodies. We were practically afraid of our own bodies. Today it's very different, there is more freedom and a much more liberated and progressive perception of the body. We also offer a lot of courses related to the body and movement, like dance and theater. In general, women demand a greater position in the public sphere. Academically, too, there aren't many religious schools where girls can major in physics and cinema and theater. We were the first. You have to understand, Kedumim is a place where women have always had a large influence. Take Daniella Weiss, for example." Weiss, a prominent activist for the settler movement, is a former mayor of Kedumim.

Eliash tells me her daughter is a member of two forums on Facebook. One is called "I'm a religious feminist and I also don't have a sense of humor," and takes a stance against harassment of women and religious Zionist leaders' silence on the subject. The second is "Halakhic Feminists." But she says the feminist question did not preoccupy her own generation at all. "Practically speaking, I was very feminist. I was the deputy chair of the Yesha Council and in many forums I was the only woman. I remember once, at a meeting, someone said it was time to give a Dvar Torah, and it didn't occur to anyone to ask me.[9] That bothered me then, but I saw it as the only extant state of affairs."

I ask Eliash if she feels her life's purpose has been fulfilled.

She looks around. "This miracle is more than anything I dreamed of achieving."

* * *

---

9 A homiletic talk based on the weekly Torah portion. It is considered a token of respect to be invited to deliver a Dvar Torah at a gathering.

Large metal posts in the middle of the road rise up and disappear again with the press of a button: the entrance to the settlement of Elon Moreh has a state-of-the-art barrier. Ha'Bayit Ha'Yehudi is holding its primaries today, and the streets are deserted. A poster of Sarah Eliash is the only visible evidence of what's happening. Elon Moreh is a fairly small community, founded in 1980 and home to some sixteen hundred people, with the hallmark red-tiled roofs found in Kedumim and other settlements. A young man wearing a black coat pushes a baby in a stroller, with an M16 rifle slung over his shoulder. He directs us to the polling booth: "Next to Birkat Yosef Yeshiva." We pass a few signs ("Shomron View Guesthouse," "Eynav's Confectionaries") and offend a young man with a boyish face by asking if he's old enough to vote. "I have three kids at home," he retorts.

Outside the polling place, a few youngsters walk around with signs, fliers, posters, T-shirts and hats with their candidates' names. Some voters are already lining up. There is no conflict between the candidates' representatives here. The young men, students from the post-secondary yeshivas in Elon Moreh and Itamar, have not chosen their candidates for ideological reasons and are not particularly vociferous campaigners. They're indifferent to the outcome. This polling location will shut by four in the afternoon and voting will move to Itamar.

Still, they are an energetic bunch, mostly in their twenties, and when I spend time with them I notice that they shout and jump around a lot, swinging between different moods, switching from a friendly to a hurt tone, frequently talking over each other. Twenty-year-old Shmuel studies at Birkat Yosef, a *hesder* yeshiva—an arrangement that allows Israelis to complete a program of religious studies as part of their extended army service. I ask if he is excited about the big day for Ha'Bayit Ha'Yehudi, which is holding its primary elections today and expecting the largest turnout in the party's history. But he's not enthused: "I don't really support them. They keep veering to the left, and they don't believe in Eretz Yisrael (the Land of Israel) like I do. I'm not willing to give away land for money, and I'm not willing to support laws against the Torah. I support this…" He turns his cell phone over to reveal a sticker: "Strength for Israel." So he's a devotee of Michael Ben-Ari, a member of Knesset who is an open disciple of the ultra-right-wing rabbi Meir Kahane, who was assassinated in 1990. The young man's face glows in anticipation of my horror at his extremist views—ultimately all adolescents are alike, I suppose.

I ask another student, Amichai, about his yeshiva studies. He describes a daily academic routine that ends at 11 p.m., and says his favorite class is with the head of the yeshiva, Rabbi Elyakim Levanon. He hands me a substantial volume of Talmudic commentary by "the Ritba" (the acronym of Yom Tov ben Avraham Asevilli), who was considered one of Spain's greatest rabbinic minds in the thirteenth century. That's what he's reading now. "The studies make me a better person," he affirms.

"How's that?"

"I'm learning how to behave, what to believe in. On the emotional level, something is breaking free, growing. I'm euphoric on the days when I study." Politically, he is unequivocal. "The two peoples are connected to the same area, we just want them to be thrown out of here."

The political divide doesn't particularly upset them, but tempers quickly flare over the discord between the students from Birkat Yosef in Elon Moreh, led by Rabbi Levanon (who are the majority here today), and some of their counterparts from the Itamar yeshiva, under Rabbi Avichai Rontzki, a former Chief Military Rabbi and today a candidate for the Knesset with Ha'Bayit Ha'Yehudi. Levanon, who was not an especially renowned rabbi before the disengagement, gained widespread support among young settlers when he took a hard line in support of soldiers refusing orders to vacate the settlers, and championed the supremacy of Eretz Yisrael (the Land of Israel) over Am Yisrael (the Jewish People). "Rabbi Levanon became well known after the disengagement," a source familiar with the *hesder* yeshiva world told me. "Up to then his yeshiva was marginal, he didn't have many students, and all of a sudden after 2005 he gained a lot of students, and since then his yeshiva has been growing. His mirror image is Rabbi Yuval Cherlow, who expressed more complex opinions at the time, including an opposition to violence, and his yeshiva was empty after 2005."

"What other differences do you see between the yeshivas?" I ask young Amichai.

"Most of the values are similar but the methods are different. The method at the Itamar yeshiva is to achieve our aims by means of connecting with Israeli society. In fact, it's like the difference between change from the outside and change from within: for us, it's about being together with the entire Jewish people, including the secular ones, acting from within, listening to secular views too. Whereas their approach is more *hardali* and isolationist—as in, we're better, we set an example and you should learn from us, we won't accept any secular influence.[10] In our yeshiva we believe that every idea contains some merit, and that it's good to disagree with the head of the yeshiva."

I ask him to expand on these complexities, for example with regards to the difference between the high-school yeshiva and the post-secondary yeshiva in this context.

"At the post-secondary yeshiva I came to understand that life is more complex. I'm more politically moderate now, too. I realize there is no solution here and now, we can't make peace and we can't kill all the Arabs. As a high-school yeshiva boy I saw things in black and white, I wanted everything here and now."

"How do you view secular Zionism?"

"Secular Zionism has more or less collapsed. They have a crisis of faith, they don't know what parts of Zionism they accept and what parts they don't. The rupture between the generations is enormous: the kids there loathe the things their parents did, like in the Mossad and the army, but they live in apartments their parents bought. They don't live according to their own values at

---

10 *Hardali* comes from the Hebrew acronym *h-r-d-l*, which stands for "National Orthodox"—the Israeli community that espouses strict religious observance but leans toward a Zionist political outlook.

all. We don't take pleasure in this, by the way, it's just a fact. Not long ago I saw a Labor Party campaign ad from 1981, where they were boasting about the large number of settlements they'd built."

"Is it possible that they've changed?"

"I don't say this because I'm religious—secular Zionism is in a crisis. What do they believe in now? What is their vision? Religious Zionism has not experienced a crisis of faith. Our goals have not changed and neither have our values."

Now I'm surrounded by the Birkat Yosef group again. I speak with a good-looking young man named Sherman. With his blue eyes and long hair, he reminds me a little of a Coke ad from the nineties, something featuring (acceptably) rebellious and photogenic teenagers. Sherman wants to write for *Haaretz*. "You know," he says gravely, "we were just talking yesterday about why we didn't take part in the Tel Aviv demonstrations about the cost of food and all that. Maybe because our lives are completely different, we're not troubled by those things. Our families don't eat out at restaurants and we don't travel abroad."

I ask this group of fifteen men in their early twenties how many of them have been overseas. Not a single hand goes up.

"You see?" Sherman continues. "We don't want to live luxurious lives. We're not interested in restaurants and apartments and cost of living. If Tel Aviv's expensive, we'll live in Kiryat Gat, or Itamar, or Kiryat Shmona."

"But you're overlooking the ideology of the protest movement," I point out. "It was largely about the divide between the rich and the poor, about income inequality, not just about how much a loaf of bread costs. Aren't you being a little reductive?"

"Just like you are about us the whole time," he laughs. "The fact that I have a big yarmulke and *tzitzit* fringes hanging out and long hair doesn't mean the purpose of my life is to beat up Arabs—"

"—even if that does happen sometimes," a friend interjects.

"He's just kidding," they assure me.

"And," Sherman adds, "the fact that I study the Torah doesn't mean I want to live off the state. I sit here wasting a lot of time, time when I could be working, making money, getting married. Because studying the Torah is the greatest purpose there is."

"Explain," I urge him.

"Our lives are the Torah. Everything stems from the Torah, and so our values are higher than those of the left wing."

Sometimes there is a noticeable discrepancy between the pathos contained in these young men's words and the tone in which they speak. It's as though they themselves have not yet completely cemented their views, or at least do not entirely grasp the severity of words in general. They're still a work in progress, and sometimes they say things simply to defy or impress. They can change their opinions from one sentence to the next, yet still believe with all their hearts that they speak the truth at any given moment. This is youth: the force of the argument and the power of persuasion, the belief that one speaks in the name of absolute truth.

I've run out of pages in my notebook. A big young man with

the broad grin of a confirmed troublemaker volunteers to buy me a new one. I give him ten shekels, and he returns a few minutes later and hands me a new notebook with a grainy brown cover, the likes of which I haven't seen since grade school. He insists on returning my change. Forget it, I tell him: it's my modest donation to Birkat Yosef Yeshiva. But he won't hear of it. Eventually we decide to buy some cookies with the remaining funds. I'm surprised by how much ten shekels can buy around here.

People regularly walk past and warn the students against *Haaretz*, which will depict them as crazy racists, against the left wing, the Tel Avivis, the secular. One particularly annoying fellow asks for a press card (which I don't have), and comments several times that these young kids "aren't even from Shomron, they just go to school here, they shouldn't talk on behalf of Shomron." Another man reminds them not to speak for the yeshiva. Yet another explains that they don't represent the yeshiva or the Shomron. Listen, I tell the last nuisance, I won't mention the word Shomron, just get out of here.

When I question the students about their political solution, a boy named Elisha approaches. "There shouldn't be any burning of Arabs or hitting of soldiers. I'll fight with all my strength, but I won't use violence. There is a difference between my treatment of Jews and Arabs: I'm more committed to the Jews, but the Arabs must understand that I am the ruler. If anyone has to be afraid around here, I'd rather the Arabs be afraid of me."

"What are the Palestinians' rights in this place?"

"Their rights are under our control. The Arabs deserve

human rights but not civil rights. They don't have to vote. Ideally, we'd prefer that they not be here. You don't understand that this is a religious war, that's the story. All wars in the world are religious wars."

"Every human being has the right to live in dignity," adds Yosef from the Itamar yeshiva, "as long as he recognizes the Jews' control of the state. The lives of the Arabs under the rule that you call occupation are very good. Are they better off in Syria? Besides, they can have their own regional councils, just like they do in Europe."

"Where?"

He doesn't know exactly. "Morality to me is that a person has the right to live in dignity, he deserves a livelihood, a job, a family and a normal life. Whoever is here we will treat with respect, but, regardless of that, the State of Israel should encourage the Arabs to emigrate."

"Where to?"

"To Arab states, to Europe. They say it'll be nice on Mars…"

Elhanan is a serious young man from the Itamar yeshiva. "To me it's a long and complicated process," he says. "There is no quick solution to a conflict that's lasted over a hundred years. Have you read Boogie Ya'alon's book, *The Long Short Road*?"

"Oh, I read it every night," I reply with a smile.

The former Chief of Staff turned leading Likud politician Moshe ("Boogie") Ya'alon published his collection of personal recollections and political analyses in 2008.

"So he writes in the book that there are two major problems:

first 'transfer,' and second the Peace Now movement. They are two extreme and inflexible modes of thought. Maybe there is no solution in our time. That's a possibility, right?"

"It's interesting that you quote Ya'alon. That means you've read his book. What books have influenced all of you?"

Two of them mention *The Long Short Road*. One names *Masa Kumta* by Elazar Stern (published in English translation, in 2012, as *Struggling Over Israel's Soul*). *Five Homilies* by Rabbi Joseph Soloveitchik. Benjamin Netanyahu's *A Place Among the Nations*. Someone else mentions *Letters to Talia*, a collection of correspondence between a religious soldier who was killed in the Yom Kippur War and a secular girl from a kibbutz in northern Israel who writes under the name Talia. And *Adjusting Sights*, a novel by Rabbi Haim Sabato that takes place during the Yom Kippur War. Perhaps more than anything else they've said, this reading list points to the disconnect between young secular Israelis and these students.

"It's because we are still excited about Zionism, it still moves us," Yosef explains.

I remember a quote from the literary critic Dov Sedan, repeated by author Amos Oz, saying that all of Zionism is no more than a passing episode, an outburst of secularism and politics that Jewish law will eventually swallow up. But the truth is that not only was Zionism not swallowed up, it has in fact expanded and adapted over the years. And the religious, messianic ideas that it always contained—redemption for the Jewish people who have returned to their land and are completing a historical continuity—have begun to take on a more vivid expression among the secular public, too. This makes sense: after all, secular Zionists today do not believe God exists, but are willing to swear that He did once hover over this place and that He gave the land to the Jewish people. Either way, in these days when the Labor Party has been reborn as "The Zionist Union," it is fairly clear that secular Israelis are still "moved by" Zionism as they interpret it. The Zionist Union's own leaders, for example, repeatedly insist that Zionism today means helping the weak and treating everyone equally.

I notice that these students often take issue with the left wing and the media, keen to dispute the way they are depicted by supposedly leftist outlets. I ask Sherman about this. "I've heard how confident you are about your status and your way of life, but at the same time you're always talking to the left wing, arguing with its perception of you. Why does that preoccupy you so much?"

"It's a trauma," he answers immediately. "They never considered us, they never took our views seriously. Mostly they made fun of our opinions after distorting them. Bottom line, does anyone care about our opinions? Does anyone really want to get to know us? God willing, eighty years from now everything will be different, and there will be a Holy Temple here." Then, seeming to sense that his reply might signal weakness and an injured pride, he changes course. "But we're the elite, even you know that in your heart."

Elhanan from the Itamar yeshiva intervenes, perhaps to underscore the explanation he gave earlier about the difference between the Itamar and Elon Moreh yeshivas. "Where does this arrogance come from? Who said we're better? Because we're religious that means we're the elite?"

Sherman insists: "Because I observe the religious commandments, I'm expected to be more moral than a secular person."

"Do you believe that Jews are more moral than Gentiles?" Elhanan asks him. "That they have a different role?"

"I do," Sherman answers.

"Then you're a racist."

"It's not that we're better," another student weighs in, "it's that we have more of a commitment, more responsibility for something greater."

"Morality is based on the Torah," Sherman says as he jumps on a friend's back. "Look, the greatest mission of our lives is to accustom our eyes to see things according to the Torah."

7

The Closest Thing to Hell
Palestinian Jerusalem beyond the Separation Wall

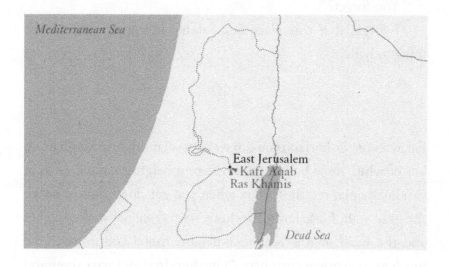

The couches in the small living room have a delicate pattern in their green upholstery, and those in the large living room are maroon. Well-dressed boys and girls run around, stopping to shake my hand or nod hello. A pretty little girl wearing a light pink hat looks out of the window, indifferent to the attention lavished upon her. Leila, the forty-five-year-old matriarch of the family, sits in the middle of the couch, flanked by her daughters:

twenty-four-year-old Wala, with a baby on her lap, and twenty-year-old Ayah, who inches her way to the far end of the couch. Leila's husband Ismail sits opposite them with his ten-year-old daughter and six-year-old granddaughter perched on the arms of his chair. Everyone is looking at him.

"When I'm at home—and I almost never leave home—sometimes I forget," says Wala as she strokes her baby, "'because the house is beautiful and neat and we've invested so much in it."

"You forget?"

"I forget that this place is a satanic invention. The closest thing to hell."

* * *

Far away on the horizon you can see a sort of miniature Manhattan: lots of white stone buildings of different heights, slanted roofs in various shapes, red tiles. Only when you get closer do you notice the gray wall. I ask Jamil Sanduka, a professional snake-catcher and the head of Ras Khamis's neighborhood committee, how much an apartment costs here. "One hundred and sixty thousand shekels (US$42,000) will get you a thirteen-hundred-square-foot apartment, including a new kitchen, anything you want," he says.

Ras Khamis and Ras Shehada are two adjacent neighborhoods in northeastern Jerusalem, not far from the predominantly Jewish neighborhood of French Hill. Like the nearby refugee camp of Shuafat, they have been located within Jerusalem's municipal borders since 1967, and most of their residents have blue identity cards—meaning they are permanent residents but not citizens of Israel. In the middle of the last decade, their lives were transformed when the so-called "security fence" was constructed, separating them from the rest of Jerusalem. Now, when residents want to pray on the Temple Mount, visit family in the Old City, work in the center of town, or seek medical treatment, they must go through the Shuafat checkpoint.

The wall surrounded these neighborhoods with a tight band, trapping their residents in a no-man's-land that lacks any clear authority. In effect, Israel created a new Palestinian domain here, the likes of which had never been seen before. The Palestinian Authority is not allowed to enter the neighborhoods because they are under Israeli sovereignty, but most Israeli officials don't venture over the wall to the Palestinian side, which is ostensibly connected to the West Bank. The people who live here are residents of Jerusalem, though there is no evidence of any municipal authorities: the city does not remove trash, rarely repairs or paves roads, and doesn't handle the sewage. If your home is burgled, there's no chance the police will respond; if you have a heart attack, don't bother waiting for an Israeli ambulance.

As a result of the changes brought about by the wall, each neighborhood established a committee to handle a broad range of matters. In the absence of municipal services or enforcement, buildings seem to spring up anywhere a resident wishes to put one. Sanduka says that anyone with minimal funds can fence off a plot of land and build on it. There are no regulations, no permits. But who, I wonder, would want to live in a neighborhood completely cut off from the city? As it turns out, demand is on the rise. In the years since the wall was built, the number of residents in these neighborhoods has grown. Israeli authorities, including the Jerusalem municipality, do not keep figures, but the population is estimated at eighty thousand residents. Why do they move here? One reason is that housing prices on the Israeli side of East Jerusalem are skyrocketing, while here a Palestinian Jerusalemite can purchase a spacious apartment for a price that would strike someone from Isawiya, for example, a neighborhood on the other side of the wall, as science fiction. But there is a trade-off: when a Palestinian moves to Ras Khamis, he will have to go through a checkpoint every time he wants to reach central Jerusalem. It's unclear if these developments were part of a brilliant scheme to rid Jerusalem's streets of Palestinians—and if so, whether or not it's working.

Driving down the main road, a pungent smell of burning trash makes it hard to breathe. Heaps of garbage tower on both sides of the road, most of it blackened. They burn trash all over this place—roughly eighty percent of all the garbage. The city stopped hauling trash a long time ago and privatized the service, but the contractor who won the bid prefers to burn it. The residents do so too. As I looked out, I was reminded of Tristan Egolf's description of a garbagemen's strike in a small American town in his novel *Lord of the Barnyard*: "To the rear and side of every building, along the outer boundaries of each lot, in the ditches, at the base of every lamppost, in the disposal pits, the break areas, on staircases and loading ramps—everywhere you looked—sprawling ranges of scrap and debris sat oozing and withering in the heat." In Egolf's dystopia, piles of trash eventually overflow, people start burning them, and the stench engulfs the entire town. In some ways Ras Khamis seems to be fulfilling the nightmarish vision depicted in this novel, one of my favorites.

We drive along a winding, potholed road full of clods of dirt. There are no sidewalks here, not a single tree or any greenery, no lampposts. A jumble of cars and pedestrians pour out of the side alleys into a small traffic jam that builds up in both directions. "When there's an accident," Sanduka tells me, "the police don't come." There are more alarming cases too: a week ago, two motorcyclists shot fourteen bullets at a man driving his car. The committee called the police, who told them to bring the victim and his vehicle to the checkpoint, since an Israeli ambulance would not cross the wall to administer care. When a resident requires urgent medical treatment, a (Palestinian) Red Crescent ambulance can take him or her as far as the wall, where Israeli paramedics can take over.

In 2005 the residents filed a Supreme Court petition against the outline of the wall and asked to remain on the Israeli side. I ask someone who sat in on the court hearings how this peculiar situation—leaving Israeli neighborhoods on the Palestinian side of the wall—was ever authorized in the first place.

"It was an interesting spectacle," he recalls. "The state attorney began explaining that the whole thing stemmed from security concerns. But the petitioners' lawyer asked, 'Which security concerns? This street here is outside the wall, and the one next to it is inside the wall. Are you saying Street A has terrorists

on it and Street B doesn't?' Then Aharon Barak, the Supreme
Court President at the time, advised the state attorney how to
proceed with his argument: 'You have, in effect, applied Israeli
sovereignty to these neighborhoods, correct? Well, then, the state
is allowed to build a wall wherever it wishes.'"

The court refused to issue an interim order to halt construction of the wall, explaining that it had "considered, among other
things, the fact that the placement of the wall does not injure the
lands of any of the petitioners."

"Technically, that is correct," explains Mohammed Dahla, a
Jerusalem lawyer who has represented various north Jerusalem
neighborhoods in similar cases. He makes his point by drawing a
comparison with a solidly Jewish neighborhood in West Jerusalem
such as Rehavia. "If they build a wall around Rehavia and put
up a barrier with guards, in effect not one yard has been taken
from residents' land. The interesting thing about this Supreme
Court case was the extent to which the judges, especially Dorit
Beinisch, delighted in the fact that the Palestinians were asking
to remain on the Israeli side of the wall. All they wanted to hear
was how much the Palestinians don't want a state but instead
want to be in Israel, which is the same tune Lieberman sings
about Palestinians in the 'Triangle.' They didn't get the point:
the petitioners wanted to be part of East Jerusalem society, just as
they always had been, because that is where they have businesses
and families, and they wanted to be close to the holy sites. We
proposed a plan devised by the Council for Peace and Security
that meets Israel's security needs. We said: You want separation

between Jews and Arabs? No problem, but don't separate the residents of these neighborhoods from East Jerusalem. Instead, move the fence so it's between East Jerusalem and West Jerusalem. Of course they denied our petition."

In 2008 the Supreme Court issued final authorization for the placement of the wall around the Shuafat Ridge neighborhoods. This time the case was heard by Dorit Beinisch, the future president Asher Grunis, and Edmund Levy. Some of the residents in question had no legal status in Israel, and the court had little trouble contending with them. But the bigger question concerned the permanent residents:

> With regards to residents of the neighborhoods on the Shuafat Ridge who possess legal status in the State of Israel, they are indeed expected to suffer injury to their right to have access to Jerusalem and move within it. But when this injury is examined against the security requirements, it is a reasonable injury. These residents' access to the rest of Jerusalem's areas is not prevented, although it is restricted; the primary restriction, which is considerable, results from the need to go through the transit terminal set up at the security barrier...The construction of the barrier creates difficulties for the residents of the Shuafat Ridge neighborhoods, including those who are permanent residents of Israel, in their transit to their places of employment...to municipal services, most of which are located in the other parts of Jerusalem...Offices of the Ministry of the Interior, the National Insurance, and the Employment Service,

which are planned to be opened near the terminal, will help to preserve the residents' access to municipal and governmental services...Against this damage, which is reducible, one must take into account the fact that the barrier fulfills the important security purpose of preventing free passage of terrorists and terrorism activists into areas of Israel.

Back at the checkpoint, I see no trace of any representatives from the Ministry of the Interior, the National Insurance, or the Employment Service. A few buses are parked in an adjacent lot, the gathering point for thousands of children who go to school in East Jerusalem every day. Sanduka usually gets up early to make sure the kids leave on time. "Every morning I get up to open the gates and send the kids off." He smiles. "On days when I'm not here, there are fights between the police and the pupils. There's always tension." Sanduka, a bulky man with a beard, gets a salary "from the bus company." Sometimes he makes a living catching snakes, which he grabs with his bare hands.

You know, I tell him, in the 1980s, Amos Oz and David Grossman traveled around the country talking with Palestinians like I'm doing, and in the books they wrote there is a lot of Palestinian black humor about the occupation. I hardly hear any of that.

He gives a wry smile. "That makes sense. Occupation humor is boring at this point. There was a time when a lot of the black humor was aimed at the new PA, but that's over too. I think there was humor when people still believed change was possible. No one's in the mood to laugh anymore."

Not even a hundred and fifty feet away, we get to the Shuafat Refugee Camp. Girls with green uniforms and backpacks walk alongside the wall on their way to school, while cars honk incessantly. The refugee camp is under Israeli sovereignty but is also supported by UN agencies, primarily UNRWA. The girls are headed to a new school in a modern building with blue framed windows. Some kids play outside in the sand, in a small yard. This school is only for camp residents, and Sanduka says that while the UN provides education for the refugee camp's kids, children from other neighborhoods have a run-down school built on land that once housed goats, near a known drug house, which we plan to visit. Most of the kids travel elsewhere.

We talk to Baha Nabata, an energetic young civil rights activist and community organizer from Shuafat, whom I have met on previous occasions. He points out a little kid climbing up a huge pile of trash holding a garbage bag, which he then tosses over the wall. Baha grins: "That's our little rebellion against Israel: we throw our garbage to the other side. But it's also so the smell doesn't suffocate us."[11]

---

11 I met with Baha Nabata several times when I visited the East Jerusalem neighborhoods where he worked. A month after our last meeting, on a Monday night, he was standing with a group of people near a road-paving project he had initiated, when a gunman fired ten bullets at him and fled. Nabata died at age thirty-one, leaving behind a wife and two daughters. The motive for his assassination has not been confirmed. He was a passionate young leader who devoted his life to improving the lot of Palestinian communities outside the separation wall.

Near the end of the street, we're back in Ras Khamis again. We pass a grocery, a falafel stand, clothing shops, a jewelry store. The car maneuvers between the potholes, and a crane swings high above us toward the shell of a new building. Abu Adham, Sanduka's counterpart in Ras Shehada, explains dismissively: "The city told us a new contractor will come to fix the road in May. But then we realized we didn't ask May of which year." Neither man is particularly interested in talking about politics, or a Palestinian state, or Israeli Arabs. They are mostly preoccupied with their own neighborhoods' affairs. They maintain constant contact with the Jerusalem authorities, fighting to win the same rights that all Jerusalemites are given. Even though they know there is likely no chance this will happen, still they insist on voicing their demand to be part of Jerusalem under Israeli sovereignty. According to the maps and to the letter of the law, after all, Ras Khamis is a Jerusalem neighborhood just like nearby Isawiya or my own childhood neighborhood of Beit Ha'Kerem.

Sanduka and Abu Adham say the city has been gradually disconnecting from these neighborhoods since 1988, but the big change occurred after the wall was built. Since then, the only municipal representatives that the residents see are the collectors who knock on doors to deliver municipal property tax bills. Anyone who doesn't pay—and many don't—could be arrested at the checkpoint. The checkpoint is a trap in many ways, hindering people's ability to move, making them rethink their daily conduct, their identity papers, their answers to questions and the time they can expect to waste in line.

The lack of law enforcement naturally increases crime rates. One local woman tells us there are weapons in every household: MAG machine guns, M16 rifles (which might cost US$14,000 but use cheap ammunition) and the Carl Gustav machine gun known in these parts as "Carlo," which is brought in from Nablus, "but it's a lousy gun." Criminals have been employing a new tactic lately: they dress up as members of the Israeli Border Patrol's special ops counter-terrorism unit ("Yamam"), complete with gear, and turn up at people's houses "to perform a search." The last person who was visited by these imposters lost more than US$50,000 and a stash of jewelry. Sanduka shows us a YouTube clip from a jewelry store's security camera, which shows a gang of burglars in Yamam outfits strolling around the store, loading their bags. "It's all because of the people from Jenin and from up north who came to the Shuafat Refugee Camp," one resident claims. "They deal arms and drugs, and because there's such chaos here they can do anything."

Indeed, there is no clear authority in these neighborhoods. The law is ambiguous, leaving people to conduct their lives based on temporary arrangements, fragile understandings and ad-hoc solutions to urgent problems. At any point someone might violate an agreement, exposing the committee leaders' lack of real power to apply sanctions. They do mediate when conflicts arise, but sometimes the facts are determined by a decisive move by one party or another. There is no genuine power here, no state or city entity making enforceable decisions.

In a fenced-off lot roughly an acre in size, tractors and

dumpsters are strewn around, and several construction workers walk through empty building shells. The land belonged to
a former resident who donated it to the city to build an elemen-
tary school. But a group of people arrived one day and took over
the land, and now they're building. The committee heads have
been chasing down municipal officials trying to get the buildings
destroyed, but the officials claim they don't have the budget to
do anything. It's difficult for the committees to keep up with the
construction pace. Sometimes a small-time developer will build
a high-rise on an unstable dirt foundation, and their greatest fear
is that one day one of these tall buildings, home to five hundred
tenants each, will collapse.

Over the years, alongside the complaints and anger directed at
the city and the state, committee members and residents have also
developed a certain sense of pride—in their accomplishments,
in the arrangements they've reached among themselves, in the
things that do work here. Sometimes what starts out as a grum-
bling description of an obstacle ends up as a happy account of a
creative solution. The construction of the wall has essentially left
these neighborhoods to fend for themselves, and they could have
easily become arenas of total chaos and violent competition over
resources—like any district lacking a police force, a municipality
and courts of law. Those indicators do exist here, but people have
joined forces to stabilize the streets and set up their own systems.
They gleefully tell the story of last winter's storm, an anomaly in
Jerusalem's climate, when snow piled up and a state of emergency
was declared. The committees managed to increase the bakeries'

output, borrow power generators from residents, clear the snow at record speed and open up the roads. They worked so efficiently that they even helped Jewish neighborhoods inside the wall, like Pisgat Zeev and Ma'ale Adumim, to clear their own roads.

Sanduka and Abu Adham show us one of the area's more notorious attractions, a drug den in an abandoned house among piles of trash. It's dark here, and at most you can see the occasional figure moving in the shadows. Sanduka says East Jerusalemites come here to buy drugs, as do soldiers, young Jerusalemites and people from all over the area. They've been talking about shutting this place down for over a decade, but it's still here. A journalist who toured the neighborhood with Sanduka reported that Israeli security forces were gathering at the checkpoint in civilian clothes, planning to visit the drug house ahead of possible action. Sanduka knew most of these security operatives by name, and he explained to them—not for the first time—about the repercussions of the drug house. When I ask if there's been any progress, he replies, "Maybe."

Sanduka and Abu Adham often meet with city officials, and they've also been to the Knesset, where they've even managed to enlist financial aid. But they've given up trying to find rhyme or reason in their successes and failures with the municipality, and can only stand by helplessly as the Israeli bureaucracy continues to ignore them. Once in a while the tables turn and the Israelis ask for a favor: a few weeks ago the police asked them to help locate two Jewish girls from Pisgat Zeev who had moved to Ras Khamis after falling in love with two local boys. The committee heads talked with the women and convinced them to go back home.

When you spend enough time here, you begin to notice that from almost any spot in the neighborhood, two things are always visible: the black water tanks on the rooftops, and the separation wall. The wall—in some places gray and in others colorfully painted, often burnt along the bottom, often topped with barbed wire—is omnipresent. No matter where you stand, it will always be peering over a row of buildings. At first it's hard to ignore the way it blocks your progress at the end of every road, and you constantly arrive at a point where it seems you're about to drive straight into it, but as the hours pass, and certainly by your second visit, you grow accustomed to it. As the saying goes: when you live by the sea, you stop hearing the waves.

At one of the neighborhood's unofficial garbage dumps, the smell of burnt trash is overpowering. You can hold your breath for a while, but eventually you have to inhale the stench. We stand atop a small hill looking out onto Jerusalem on the Israeli side of the wall. Downhill are massive piles of burnt trash. This is where trucks come after collecting garbage from the entire district, offload their hauls and burn everything. The dump is adjacent to the wall, which in this stretch is as black as tar. There is an improvised bridge made of wooden planks perched on the piles, leading to a ladder propped up against the wall. This is the "night passage," where residents walk through the heaps of garbage at night, make their way over the bridge, climb up the wall, and land in Jerusalem.

We make our way through the pungent smoke, and when we emerge we are almost at the checkpoint. Looking back, we see the same horizon we observed before, but from the other side. Sanduka complains about the rampant construction, but when he observes his neighborhood's skyline he is also pleased with how it's booming, and excitedly points out the beauty of various buildings. In a yard next to us, people are busy with a large water barrel; above them, shreds of Brazilian and Italian flags flap in the wind, remnants of World Cup excitement. Kids run around, some curious and others ignoring us, until their mothers shoo them away. I observe two people pumping water, which brings us to another critical issue. Like every other area of life here, the water predicament has prompted a system of arrangements that has evolved over time. Every building has a water barrel that is filled each night for use the next day, since water is available at night but not always in the morning. People who live on or near the ground floor don't have to worry much, but on the higher floors it's a different story: a tractor comes to fill the barrels with water, which must then be pumped upstairs, requiring equipment that costs about US$180 and serves three or four stories. Sanduka estimates that for every four hundred gallons of water, they pay US$65 in auxiliary costs.

* * *

I've been wanting to meet Riad Juliani for a long time. I've heard a lot about him and seen the results of his work everywhere, but only on my last visit to Ras Khamis, a year after I first went there, does he suddenly emerge from behind a green dumpster. And there he stands, right in front of me, while a mound of rubbish burns a few feet away: the man appointed by the city to oversee sanitation and garbage removal. Resisting a quip about his name, I seize the opportunity to ask: Are you the man responsible for trash removal?

His glare soon gives way to a twitch of a smile, and it's obvious to me that we are both keenly aware of the irony of the moment. Debating how to respond, he finally goes on the offensive. "They're liars! All the committee members! I just put a huge dumpster out here and people came out with sticks and chased me away. One guy turned a dumpster into a swimming pool for his kids."

"Why do you burn trash instead of removing it?"

"Me? Am I the one burning trash? Is it the contractor I hired? It's the residents who burn it! There are eighty-five hundred tax-payers here, and that's the number we based our trash-removal tender on, but how many people actually live here? Seventy thousand. Just a month ago my clan got into a fight with two other clans who were burning garbage cans. There was shooting, knives, you name it."

"Maybe the city needs a bigger budget?"

"I asked them, they refused." He mentions a section of road about six hundred feet long in the middle of the neighborhood, which the city recently repaired. He looks at the residents gathering around us, clearly aware that most of them loathe him and view him as a collaborator with the discriminatory state establishment. "Look, I live here too, I can't breathe either, and I'm telling you: this is the worst place in the entire Middle East. In Syria it's much better."

Four schoolgirls listen to our conversation. They want to talk with me, but they won't give their names. They live in the Shuafat Refugee Camp.

"We don't recognize Israel," one declares. "The Jews take care of themselves and they leave the Arabs with the trash."

"They should give back our lands and stop threatening us with weapons, then maybe there'll be peace."

One girl seems taken aback when I ask about their pastimes. "When we want to do something fun? We go to the water park in Jericho."

Three of them want to be doctors when they grow up. The other says she'll be a history and geography teacher.

"We hate living here," says the one who wants to be a doctor of biology, "but we won't leave Jerusalem."

Back at Leila and Ismail's home, Leila says she is fearful every time Ismail goes to a demonstration. Even as we speak, he is facing charges of assaulting an officer after he led a demonstration of local residents to commemorate Nakba day. She tries to dissuade him from taking part in these events, but he doesn't listen, and then he gets arrested and she has to come up with US$1,300 for bail. Leila and her daughters remember a time before the wall was built, when their lives were focused around East Jerusalem and everything was nearby. Now, "Our lives are the identity card.

You need it at the checkpoint, you need it everywhere you go, we even sleep with our identity cards." They only rarely venture into East Jerusalem, usually to pray at al-Aqsa. When they do leave the neighborhood, they're afraid Jews will harass them because they wear the hijab. Not long ago, two of their friends were attacked at the Malcha mall in West Jerusalem. Wala says she doesn't leave home much, and after school her children stay at home or at her parents' place. She doesn't let them go out alone because she's afraid of criminals, afraid the army might arrest them, afraid of the perilous road, the black smoke. Besides, what would they do outside?

"Where would you like to live?" I wonder.

"Maybe in Ramallah," Wala answers, "everything's green there."

Aya, who sits to one side and does not speak much, recently had a miscarriage, which her mother says was because she inhaled tear gas shot by soldiers. Both sisters married at fifteen and do not work, although they sometimes sew dresses and other accessories to sell around the neighborhood. But Wala's daughter wants to be a dentist.

When I ask them about the future, Wala says, "The Jews are guests here, but if they give us our rights we will live with them in peace." She looks at her father as she speaks.

"Why are you looking at him?" I ask.

She laughs and doesn't answer. Aya clarifies: "They need to leave all of Palestine. It's enough, we don't want them here anymore."

I ask the family about something else. It seems to me that in the 1990s there was goodwill on the Palestinians' part, because Arafat had returned from exile and there was a lot of hope and big changes, which led to a willingness to compromise, even on significant things like the 1948 borders. But that era is over, and today there is no more compromising.

Ismail says it's true, the Palestinians no longer believe anything can happen with Israel, and they've returned to the most unyielding positions. They've realized they must not give in to Israel on anything. He sees three distinct periods: Oslo and the great hope it generated, the violent era of the Second Intifada, and the relative calm of the past few years.

"How do you explain this calm?"

"The Third Intifada is a matter of time," Leila answers, and Ismail adds that the West Bank is becoming more sympathetic to Hamas and to ISIS: ISIS is already here, he contends. "Sometimes I contemplate the future and I am filled with dread," says Leila. "The rest of the time I repress it, just like the trash around here."

* * *

By the afternoon, the air has cooled and there's a drizzle of rain. I look out at the gray separation wall and at a row of white highrises in the neighborhood of Kafr 'Aqab. The plaza in front of us is full of people—men, women, young and old—who appear from every direction, hurrying toward the Kalandia checkpoint. We squeeze our way into the line and quickly pass through a turnstile, which channels us toward another one. It's crowded but the line moves at a good clip. "They don't check people leaving Israel," a young Palestinian standing next to us laughs, "but on the other side—that's where it gets messy." We'd hired a yellow Palestinian cab to take us to Kafr 'Aqab, the biggest Jerusalem neighborhood located outside the wall. Its status is similar to that of Ras Khamis and Ras Shehada, except that Kafr 'Aqab residents who want to reach Jerusalem must cross at Kalandia, which is a more significant obstacle.

Kafr 'Aqab is one big maze. Crowded buildings, nameless streets, no signs, narrow lanes full of mud and sewage, broken stoplights, and new building skeletons everywhere. The black water tanks on the rooftops remind me of Ras Khamis, and in fact of every other Palestinian neighborhood. There are sixty-five thousand people living here, and in the coming year some five thousand more are expected to move in. Kafr 'Aqab is an interesting case, since part of it is within the Jerusalem municipality and the other part is in the PA's jurisdiction. The border between them is not entirely clear. Next to a fairly new school run by the PA is a mosque, and the house next to the mosque is part of Jerusalem—namely, it's Israeli. So does the mosque constitute the border? Perhaps the quality of the roads might give some indication of which state one is located in; there is a marked difference between the bumpy, potholed, sewage-lined streets of Israeli Kafr 'Aqab and the smoother surfaces one finds upon entering the PA.

Kids are burning trash cans nearby, but Abu Ashraf, the head of Kafr 'Aqab's committee, doesn't bother reprimanding them.

"We're in the PA's domain now," he explains. "If we were six hundred feet away, I'd be calling their parents."

Abu Ashraf, a white-haired man in his fifties with a trim gray beard, lives on a street lined with large, well-manicured, detached houses, which are all owned by his family. Two pictures hang on the wall of the expensive foyer in his own home: one of Sheikh Ahmed Yassin, and another of a young man with glasses and a small beard. The latter is Abu Ashraf's son, who is serving time in Ramon Prison. I ask why he's in prison, but Abu Ashraf does not want to discuss it.

He and his family used to live in the Old City, but they wanted a less crowded neighborhood with fresh air and open space. Shortly after they moved, Israel built the wall and they found themselves outside of Jerusalem. "I've been the committee chair for two and a half years," Abu Ashraf brags, and reminds us not to speak Hebrew on the street. "There were twelve thousand of us eight years ago, and now there are sixty-five thousand residents. You can buy a thirteen-hundred-square-foot three-bedroom apartment here for US$65,000, but just like in Ras Khamis, there's no infrastructure, no fire department, no municipality." Like other committee chairs we meet, he can recount many tribulations with the Jerusalem municipality. There are seventeen schools in the district and, after much lobbying on his part, the city took responsibility for three of them. The other fourteen are private, but the Ministry of Education pays their teachers' salaries.

Kafr 'Aqab is located precisely on the border between Israel and Palestine, and all the tensions converge in this neighborhood.

Sometimes Abu Ashraf seems equally sick of both sides. More than a Palestinian or an Israeli citizen, he defines himself as a Jerusalemite, and it is this primary identity that he fights for. "I informed Israel and Palestine that we are living between the two states here, and I told them: I am first of all a Jerusalemite."

There are two main categories of residents living in the areas we have toured: the first includes all the Jewish residents and a minority of the Palestinians, those who have Israeli citizenship; the second includes the remaining Palestinians, who are devoid of civil rights and subject to the whims of a Jewish regime that controls them through various legal and bureaucratic means. But the Palestinian neighborhoods outside the wall constitute a third (and, admittedly, inventive) category, in which Palestinians carry Israeli permanent resident cards but in actuality do not live within the State of Israel. They are connected to areas under the PA's jurisdiction (it's easier for them to reach Ramallah than East Jerusalem) but legally they have no link to the PA. They are Jerusalemites who do not, officially, live in Jerusalem.

Abu Ashraf's chief concern is the Kalandia checkpoint, which makes the locals' lives a nightmare. "We had a meeting with the commander of the checkpoints, and I told him: 'This transit point is a lie to the Jews and a horrible punishment for the Palestinians.'"

"Why is it a lie to the Jews?"

"Because you go through the checkpoint, they examine you, they humiliate you, and then three hundred feet away you can buy a knife with a twenty-inch blade for twenty shekels."

"How many Palestinians from Kafr 'Aqab go through Kalandia every day?"

"Many thousands," he says. "And tens of thousands of other people want to, but they've just given up, or else their rights were taken away from them deceptively. The soldiers at the checkpoint are always playing with us, firing shots in the air, shutting down the checkpoint, yelling at us. Three thousand eight hundred of our students pass through there every day."

"How difficult is it to get through?"

"You'll see," he scoffs.

Evening is considered the time of day when traffic through Kalandia is at its lightest; the big rush is in the morning, when Palestinian laborers who work in Jerusalem have to get through. We crowd in under a shelter alongside dozens of men and women. It's quiet and tense, and almost no one talks. The cab driver who brought us here, an Israeli resident with a blue ID card, told us he spent his whole life in West Jerusalem, but now he has no transit permit and he hasn't seen the city in four years. "At the checkpoint, you're always focused on one thing," he says, "will they let you through or will there be trouble? It's the humiliation, the uncertainty. You have no control over your day-to-day."

We stand in line to get to an iron turnstile. Every so often we hear a loud beep and three people walk through the turnstile, which immediately locks behind them. The three who get through stand in a sort of holding area, and one by one they go up to a window and present their ID cards. If their papers are in order, they must take off their coats, belts, and sometimes shoes, and put them through a scanner along with their bags. If another beep sounds and a red light goes on, they also remove their shirts and put them in the machine. It takes a few minutes for three people to get through, but if the soldiers find a problem with the papers, the process can drag on for fifteen minutes. It's been almost an hour and we're close to the gate now, with a line of about eighty people stretching behind us. In the morning, that number can reach up to a thousand.

When our turn finally comes, we walk through the turnstile and approach the soldiers, who inform us that we've broken the law: Jews are not allowed to be in Area A.

"But we weren't in Ramallah," I explain. "We were in Jerusalem."

"What do you mean, Jerusalem?!" The soldier is getting annoyed. "You were on the Palestinian side, that's a criminal offence."

"We were in Jerusalem," I repeat. "According to the law and the maps we did not leave Jerusalem."

"Jerusalem is there." The soldier points to the left.

"But also here." I point to the right.

The soldier says he'll check. Meanwhile, we're stuck in the holding area between the turnstile and the gate to Jerusalem. Two smartly dressed young Palestinian men stand around with us, having been told by the same soldiers to wait. They don't complain, just glance at us every so often. The Palestinians know that one wrong word or a misinterpreted look at a soldier could get them kicked back out to the other side.

I look back at the Palestinians crowded behind the turnstile and contemplate the way Israelis have changed their perspective over the years. In the eighties and, even more so, after the First Intifada, many Israelis were horrified by the occupation and the conduct it entailed—daily abuses, killings, systematic oppression. But now the occupation routine has become normalized for the vast majority of Israeli society. We no longer see that a sophisticated society of jailers has risen up here, in which the finest talents, resources and military might are directed toward improving the methods of controlling millions of Palestinians who are trapped in two giant prisons—a slightly malleable one in the West Bank, and a harsher one in Gaza—whether by soldiers at an old-fashioned checkpoint or by means of new inventions manufactured by high-tech companies like Elbit Systems.

The reasons for this inability to see are varied: desperation, habituation, lack of faith in a political resolution. Most Israelis alive today were born into this reality and have never known a different one, and a very large number of them are complicit in the preservation and enhancement of the oppression. But something else has happened, too: in the eighties, the appalled reactions to the occupation stemmed partly from fear of the effects it would have on Israeli society; those warning signs were articulated most pointedly by the philosopher Yeshayahu Leibowitz. Today everyone seems to understand that the occupation has indeed seeped into the foundation of our lives in Israel. Whether we like it or not, we live in a society molded by its influence.

Another reason for the dulled sense of horror is that people see no political reality that could change the situation. And when horror is accompanied by continual helplessness, it naturally abates. Concerns about the morality of Israeli society were gradually replaced by a different debate, one that was always present but which, in the past decade, has become the left wing's main rallying call: international opinion. The core of this argument is that the world will never accept the occupation, that Israel will pay a heavy price and it should therefore be stopped. The Labor Party is the most prominent mouthpiece of this position. The left wing's reliance on "the world" to bolster its argument is so great that if the international community were suddenly to announce that it accepts the occupation and the wall and the Kalandia checkpoint, the entire Israeli left wing would be silenced. What would remain, perhaps, is the fear of an Arab state.

The soldier made an effort to involve his superiors in my case, but after a while he lost interest and let me go through. Exiting the checkpoint, one feels immediate relief and a physical letdown of tension. The two young Palestinians also smile and talk among themselves, lighting cigarettes. On the other side we find many Kafr 'Aqab residents who have finished their workdays in Israel and are hurrying to get back home through the checkpoint. Somewhere out there beyond the wall, among the new towers, we can see flashpoints and hear sounds of gunfire. "Who knows?" one of the young Palestinians says as he rearranges his fur collar. "Could be trouble, or just a wedding."

Moving away from Kalandia and the line of people, which has grown much longer now, I think about Raja Shehadeh, the Palestinian lawyer and writer who has devoted most of his life to a legal battle against the occupation and the phenomena it has spawned, like the one I just witnessed at Kalandia. Shehadeh views the Oslo accords as a disaster, in which the Palestinians effectively accepted Israel's right to settle in the West Bank by consenting to the invention of "Area C," which is the largest land category in the West Bank and remains entirely under Israeli control. In his book *Palestinian Walks*, Shehadeh writes:

My weapon was the law. All my time was taken up with it. Nothing was more important. I had no doubt that if we tried hard we would win and justice would prevail. For that glorious day of liberation there was no limit to what I was willing to sacrifice. Now after Oslo was signed and the struggle as I saw it was betrayed, I was back to real time. And with its re-entry into my life, my dead father's reproachful voice was also returning...Why have you wasted your life?...What has your struggle achieved? Where did it get you? You never listened to me when I predicted the future.

8

You Can't Sweep a Tiger under the Rug

Otniel Yeshiva, Gush Etzion

The dining room at Otniel, a *hesder* yeshiva in South Mount Hebron on the West Bank, took me back to my childhood. The long crowded tables, old utensils, tasteless food, sliced whole-wheat bread, laughter and talk blending into a sort of unrelenting hum, all reminded me of my years at a WIZO daycare center. That was where I lost my sense of taste; when I got to the army, where everyone complained about the concoctions we were served in the mess hall, I could scarcely believe my luck: instead of gizzards on a bed of congealed mashed potatoes, we got free schnitzel, chicken, rice and hummus!

It's a bright day, and we decide to eat outside, where the Hebron mountains glimmer in the sun. A gang of cats leap onto our tables to grab our food. I lazily cut my meatball into pieces in the hopes one of them will snatch it, but they prefer Yakov Nagen's offerings.

Nagen is a thin, bearded man with an American accent and a great faith in the beautiful days ahead. His smile is constant, both when he is pleased and when he gets irritated, a habit that makes it difficult to interpret his intentions. He was born in Manhattan, in 1967, to an upper-middle-class family—his father was a professor of physics and his mother a lawyer—and studied at Yeshiva University. He came to Israel in 1993, attended Har Etzion Yeshiva, and for the past eighteen years has taught at Otniel Yeshiva. His wife is the head of a pre-military college for girls, and they have seven children. It's fair to say that Nagen is not your average *hesder* yeshiva teacher: he writes a New Age column for NRG, the website of one of Israel's mainstream daily newspapers, he authored a book entitled *Waking to a New Day: A Renewed Reading of the Torah and of Life,* and his interests include the Breslow branch of Hasidism, Neo-Hasidism, Buddhism, Israeli culture, and of course the teachings of Rabbi Menachem Froman, the late chief rabbi of the settlement of Tekoa, who initiated several inter-faith initiatives between Jews and Palestinians and whose spirit prevails at Otniel.

Before leaving the dining room, we stop at a memorial wall next to the kitchen. There are photographs here of very young faces. In December 2002, at the height of the Second Intifada, two terrorists infiltrated the yeshiva's kitchen through the back door. A few students were on kitchen duty and dozens of others were eating and dancing out in the dining room. Nagen recalls that, when the shooting started, the kitchen door to the dining room was locked and the terrorists could not break it down, despite heavy gunfire. When the security forces arrived, they found the body of Noam Apter, a beloved student of Nagen's, next to the door. He had apparently managed to lock it before he was killed, thereby saving his fellow students. Three other students died in the attack.

The study hall is a large, stately room with chairs and wooden desks arranged in rows, and book-lined walls. It is full of students who have just finished their lunch. Some study alone, others sit in small groups whispering to one another, or walk back and forth carrying huge hardcover books. A few are gathered around a desk listening to their teacher, whose voice ebbs and flows. A young man with curly hair, a hipster beard, headphones and an arrogant, bored look, darts past us and soon reappears lugging a book almost half his size. Pale yellow mountains and green hills are visible all around us through the large windows, with a backdrop of blue sky.

More traditional yeshivas lambast Otniel for speaking "secularish" or "Israeli-New-Age-ish." When I point this out to Nagen, he takes it as a compliment. He is not a big fan of the old-fashioned, hierarchical yeshivas that employ "a closed symbolic language." To him, the yeshiva's connection with Israeli culture, including its secular aspects, is a given. Indeed, when I ask a few students about the books they're reading, I immediately notice the difference between them and the students from Elon Moreh and Itamar whom I met earlier. The canon here is a hodgepodge: Rabbi Kook alongside Tolstoy, Amos Oz, *The Matrix*, Thomas Mann and even the Beatniks. In this yeshiva, Nagen says, they want to hear different ideas and encourage ideological disagreement. For example, one of the students recently wrote a prayer for "our brothers in the Syrian civil war," which they all learned.

Nagen expounds on his pedagogic approach: "I begin every lesson by noting the date, and then I say, 'This is the day which the Lord hath made; we will rejoice and be glad in it.' [Psalms 118:24] I stand facing life and I see that it is joy, and that the joy is present in life just as it is, and that it is the being. But reality is also flawed and difficult and frustrating, and so we must find a balance between doing and being." He quotes "some French philosopher" who said that "the challenge in life is not to discover new lands, but to see old lands in a new light." Nagen eventually remembers the name: one Marcel Proust.

"How would you define your educational philosophy?" I ask.

"To live a different life," he replies unhesitatingly. "I blend together extremely divergent ideas, including Hasidism, Kabbalah, spiritualism. I want to create balance between the spiritual worlds and the concrete worlds. But don't get me wrong," he adds, and his voice hardens briefly, "spiritualism in *hesder* yeshivas is a rising wave. The year 2000 was the year 5760 in the Hebrew calendar, and that was 'the sixties' for the national-religious sector. They did not engage with the Zohar, with Rebbe Nachman of Breslow, with the Baal Shem Tov, with spiritual methods, with imagination. What's special about our yeshiva is that we combine classical studies, namely *Halakhah* (Jewish law), with everything else. Look," he continues, "Zionism claimed to represent a return to action, and I believe that an intellectual bent that avoids isolating itself inside Judaism is a very important component, which should be rehabilitated and promoted. In the world of *hesder* yeshivas today, there is a clear trend toward the emotion and the imagination, bringing together internal components of life with the external conditions."

There are rabbis who speak out against this mingling of the religious and the secular, which they view as infiltrating yeshivas under all sorts of guises and making the religious world shallower, turning everything into a "lite" version. Here is what Rabbi Chaim Navon wrote about Nagen's version of "the sixties":

> It is difficult to ignore the prominent trend of imitating the sixties' atmosphere in America. In the sixties, we were busy building the country, and we ignored those peculiar Americans' nonsense. Now we are witnessing the sixties' sweet revenge. Long-haired and barefoot, our flower children gather...There is so much imitation and so much pretense in this belated flicker of hippieness.

"Lots of things that Otniel Yeshiva represents have moved from the margins into the center," Nagen responds. "Once, people who took an interest in more secular things were considered odd-balls, anomalies. Now it's the mainstream. Ordinary kids look to Hasidism and Kabbalah and secular Western culture. When I taught at Har Etzion Yeshiva, if someone asked a question when the head rabbi was teaching, everyone would be up in arms about a young man expressing skepticism." He adds a jab at his adversaries: "Unlike them, we encourage open-mindedness, we encourage people to learn from all worlds."

Roughly four hundred students are currently enrolled at Otniel Yeshiva, some of whom are actively serving in the IDF. The yeshiva was founded in 1987 by graduates of Ha'Kotel Yeshiva in Jerusalem's Old City, and it became a *hesder* yeshiva in the early nineties. Tuition costs more than three hundred dollars a month, which is not cheap at all. They tell me that government spending cuts, especially those made by Netanyahu in his role as Minister of Finance, hit them hard, and tuition subsidies shrank. In addition to paying tuition, these young men must meet strict academic requirements, with endless days of studying. Naturally, people here tend to come from well-off families. Yedidia is a good example: twenty-three years old, he is from Har Nof, a predominantly ultra-Orthodox neighborhood on the western outskirts of Jerusalem, and has been studying here for five years. He is a contemplative young man who considers his words before speaking, but he has a sort of youthful fervor that propels him to the big issues; he sometimes reminds me of the students who hung out in the cafeteria at Tel Aviv University, fresh from a lecture on Walter Benjamin. Yedidia is an avid reader and writer who says he prefers fiction to the history and war books favored by most of the national-religious sector.

"What works have influenced you?" I ask.

"Almost anything affects me," he replies. "I very much like Tolstoy's historic viewpoint and poetic expression, and I like [Amos] Oz's and [David] Grossman's Hebrew. I also liked *Fight Club*, and, you might be surprised, *World Shadow*—[your novel] expresses a sort of profound demand to dismantle the world we live in. I read American writers like Chabon and Franzen and others. I also read Haredi magazines and *Haaretz*. Everyone here reads things like that, but I have an especially broad sphere of engagement."

All the students I talk with proudly emphasize their yeshiva's uniqueness and voice a polite scorn for the traditional yeshivas, which they view as old-fashioned. Yedidia also maintains that Otniel is an anomaly: "You'll find that people here read less Boogie Ya'alon and more writers. I write poems and stories and cultural criticism."

"Are you a political person?"

"Ultimately, politics to me is this question: What do you want out of the world? I believe the political is existential here. A person must understand the significance of Jewish return to this place, not only to the Holy Land but to the entire Middle East. For example, how do you respond to the culture around you? What do you have to say to your neighbors? What can you learn from them? The solution to the conflict is unclear to me, but this idea that we should part company and each go our separate way seems silly. And that's the notion at the basis of the disengagement. To me, the question is how do Palestinians and Jews live together."

Yakov Nagen and I walk down the yeshiva hallways together. The basketball court outside is empty. I ask if it ever gets used, and he starts to describe a boisterous game that was played here once. This man is clearly not a sports expert. In my many conversations with Otniel's students and teachers, I scarcely hear a word about the left wing and how it controls the world.

"You live here in Otniel as a settler," I say to Nagen, "surrounded by a Palestinian population that views you as an occupier who enjoys the protection of the IDF. Doesn't that conflict with your beatific theories?"

He seems taken aback by my question. "The root of the Israeli–Palestinian conflict is not the Jews' presence in Judea and Samaria. I disagree with the assumption that our presence in Judea and Samaria, both as settlers and as an army, is what creates the problem. The IDF is in Judea and Samaria as a result of the conflict, it is not the reason for the conflict. The way I see it, the withdrawal from Gaza proves that: they took all the settlers and all the IDF soldiers out, and things are still bad for Jews and Arabs together. To my mind, separating the populations cannot constitute a real solution to the conflict."

Then Nagen remembers something he wants to show me on his computer. I protest: it's so nice out here, do we have to go back in? But he insists. Inside, he shows me a picture of himself hugging an Arab sheikh. "Every year Google makes a video summarizing the past year," he explains and his face glows. "In 2014, this was the only picture they chose from the Middle East. It was taken at an annual event called 'Jerusalem Hug,' where Jews and Arabs hug the Wall and each other. The caption they gave it was: 'It makes sense.' The clip got thirty million views."

It's hard to resist his burst of enthusiasm, and I make a point of looking at the picture for an entire minute, remembering how in Beijing they taught me that when a Chinese businessman hands you his card you must examine it thoroughly on both sides; if you just shove it in your pocket straight away, he writes you off. The photograph is a lead-in for Nagen's primary concern in recent years: Islam. "I've always been interested in religions," he says. "I started a little with Sufis in Nazareth, in Jerusalem, in Acre, but with the Sufis we live in peace. So I read the Koran a few times, and it's full of beautiful things about the perception of man and the perception of morality. A very impressive book. I invited an Egyptian scholar to the yeshiva, who wrote his doctoral dissertation about the status of Jews in the Koran, and he got a standing ovation here. Then we prayed together at the Cave of the Patriarchs. That is the future I see. In general, relations between settlers and Arabs are far more complex than what Tel Avivis who've never been over the Green Line believe. It's not just uprooted olive trees and shootings here; the picture is far more complicated. There is also a lot of love and solidarity. Rabbi Froman says that God can separate people and He can also bring them together. And I believe that the human, religious encounter is key to everything. When I meet a Palestinian and see how much he loves God, the same God I love—all the barriers fall away."

"These are lovely sentiments, and I hear them a lot in your yeshiva. So your vision is religious peace, everyone living happily together simply because they love the same God. It's hard to find a historical precedent, though, when this solution has actually worked. What are the political practicalities of this kind of peace?"

"I want to take the commonalities between the religions—we pray to the same God and we are all descendants of Abraham— and bring them into actualization."

"You describe a wonderful inter-religious harmony, with all the children of God living in peace. Everyone would like to believe in that, but if you examine the world these days, where exactly is this happening?"

"I live here and I take an interest in people who believe in this land, and I belong to several groups of Jews and Muslims who meet all the time," Nagen replies somewhat cryptically.

"Okay, then describe the principles of religious peace."

"These are the principles: One, opposition to violence. Two, it is a religious value to live in peace with one's neighbors. Three, Islam and Judaism believe in the same God. Four, we must live in a society with fully equal civil rights between Jews and Arabs. Five, recognize the Palestinian religious and historical connection to the holy land."

"And how do the settlers respond to this plan? Particularly to the fifth item, which is the most far-reaching of them all, isn't it? You are denying the Jewish people's unique and exclusive affinity with its historical homeland."

"Some of the settlers have already got as far as four, and they'll accept five in the end too," Nagen replies confidently. Once again I get the feeling that his soft-spoken and distracted nature cloaks the fervent determination of a man with a clear purpose. "Mount Hebron is not Efrat and it's not Gush Etzion—both bourgeois places. I meet with people all the time, and give lectures, and I don't see a very strong resistance. Ultimately, it is possible. It's like the religious public's move from reading *Hatzofeh*, which is a conservative bourgeois paper, to *Makor Rishon*, which offers far more challenging opinions and features cogent writing about the ideas I've presented."

"So you're also saying there is a big change among the settlers, which secular Israelis do not see?"

"Yes. Unequivocally."

"You know," I tell him, "the feeling I'm getting here is that, in the big picture, you are a one-state advocate."

"Rabbi Froman used to say that the left wing's Jewish state is a Western state, completely separated from all its neighbors. I don't want that. I wouldn't want to revoke the state's Jewish character, but if we allow equal space for another identity, nothing will happen. My direction might be the confederation direction, so that each side can preserve its identity. I'm not a political philosopher, but the one-state idea that has also been voiced in *Makor Rishon* strikes me as reasonable, and it's possible that we are being set on that course by natural motion."

The yeshiva is quiet now, shortly before the afternoon prayers. In the study hall on the first floor, and on the overlooking gallery, about two hundred students wearing yarmulkes, hats or bandanas stand in prayer. The hush is pierced by the occasional whisper or call. Some pray devoutly, rocking back and forth, while others stand motionless and stare into space. I join two students out on the large balcony. Assuming they must be scofflaws, I ask for a cigarette, but there's no smoking here. I stand looking out at the view: lots of grazing pastures and a few houses to our right, and further away the blue-gray sky over a strip of mountains dotted with plants and trees. That's all I can see when the sun is so blinding.

One of the students on the balcony is named Shahar; he's also been here for five years, and, like Yedidia, Nagen and others, he uses words like "meaningfulness," "empowerment," and "spirituality," which together with the landscape around us jog memories of times I spent with Israeli backpackers in Rajasthan. Shahar studied yoga in Jerusalem, and leads a yoga class each week before the compulsory lesson with the head of the yeshiva. In his opinion, yoga helps with concentration and can sharpen the attention to and awareness of complicated processes occurring in the human soul, which allows him and his classmates to experience the teachings in full force.

"You've been here for five years: don't you want to see the world?"

"I like being here. In this place, the Torah is not estranged from life but magnifies it. It has a spine and doesn't just follow every new fashion. It's true even when I study the Sabbath customs: when society talks about the Sabbath, its worldviews are exposed. I'll go out into the world eventually, but after a place like this the world looks more complex. Not long ago I was at a meeting with Muslims from the village of Yatta. I suddenly understood the conflict on a human level, the most distilled level. I realized that living together, with equality between people who at the end of the day share the same God, might be less impossible than it seems."

I have to laugh. "Is everyone here a lefty?"

"It's not the left wing and the right wing that everyone knows and that all the politicians talk about," Shahar explains. "We're not on the left in terms of separation. We really live here with Muslims."

This is not a place where you will hear about Jewish supremacy or suspicion of the Arabs, as you would in many settlements. But sometimes it seems that all this talk about fraternity and co-operation disguises an unwillingness to stand behind clear political ideas, the kind that entail a price. For example, the meaning of the one-state idea is that Jewish sovereignty would be threatened. One can support the idea or oppose it, but one cannot refuse to recognize its potential consequences. But in Otniel I have yet to hear any clear answers on the subject.

Afternoon prayers are over. A few of the students leave the study hall, while others go back to their lessons. Something troubles me, and I look for Yakov Nagen again. Downstairs, where the offices are located, I'm offered tea and cookies but I can't find Nagen. I get slightly lost in the long hallways, and eventually find him at the same outdoor table where we sat in the morning. The cats are gone. A group of students nearby are busy with hula hoops, streamers and other props; I can't tell if they're doing gymnastics or some sort of installation.

I explain to Nagen that we haven't delved into the future much. "You like imagination, don't you? So why don't we imagine this single state together?"

Nagen is less fond of discussing concrete plans but, being a generous man, he attempts an answer. "Not long ago I sat with a sheikh, who said to me: 'You understand the root of the problem—there is a perception that what is mine is not yours, and what is yours is not mine. But what if something that is yours… is mine?' Don't such things exist in the world? That is the failure of Oslo: a western, secular idea that did not examine any religious elements and did not examine the option for a shared life. For twenty years they've been trying to influence us from the top down, to build fences and divide up the land, A and B and C. But the truth is this: the Palestinians aren't excited about two states, they don't want fences and checkpoints. They want freedom, and that is why they talk about one state."

"The Jews are less enthusiastic," I point out.

"That's temporary," Nagen insists. "I've met with lots of Jews and Palestinians recently, and we do talk about a single state." A spark lights up his eyes. "And we gradually begin to understand: imagine that the Jews and Palestinians were to build a state together. Can you even comprehend what an empire we would be in the Middle East? In the whole world?"

* * *

On the road to Gush Etzion, the fog is so thick that we can barely make out the traffic jam. We pass the tunnel checkpoint, our fourth of the morning after Hawara, Hizmeh and another one whose name I forget. We've been driving around the occupied territories for almost a year and I still can't keep them straight; every time we take a trip, it seems like a new checkpoint I haven't seen before pops up. The memory of blue skies from South Mount Hebron belongs to a different season. The hills around us are immersed in a mist that conceals their folds and smooths them into one mass. Near the Gush Etzion winery, the sky turns overcast and it gets very cold. A few days ago there was snow on the ground here, and white clumps still dot the fields. We drive off the main road onto a rutted dirt track, park next to a few other cars and falter over the deep, soft mud into a large field covered with weeds. There is a bank of solar panels in the middle, and behind them stands a huge barn built with wooden beams. Inside, a group of people sit around a massive brick stove.

We are in "The Field." The man who owns this land, forty-two-year-old Ali Abu Awwad, inherited it from his father. Ali's parents were expelled from the Lachish region in the '48 war and settled in the nearby village of Beit Ummar. His mother was a well-known Fatah activist and spent a few years in Israeli prisons.

Ali himself served time in the early nineties, where he formulated his philosophy of non-violent resistance to the occupation. His brother was killed by IDF soldiers in the Second Intifada. Ali has dedicated the land he inherited to a fascinating project. First, together with partners from the young generation of Palestinian leadership, he is laying the foundation for a non-violent opposition movement in the spirit of Gandhi, Martin Luther King, Jr. and Nelson Mandela. Second, he has joined with Jewish partners to foster an initiative named "Roots," which provides meeting space for Palestinians and Israelis, particularly those who live in the area. The circle includes settlers from Gush Etzion and its environs, a few students of Rabbi Menachem Froman (who died in 2013), the poet Eliaz Cohen, who is a member of Kibbutz Kfar Etzion, several local Palestinians and one American pastor.

Today's meeting is in memory of Myron Joshua's mother, who died thirty days ago. Myron, a central activist in the group who lives in Kfar Etzion, talks about his mother while everyone listens intently. The only sound is the crackling of logs in the stove. Afterwards, the Jews and Palestinians cook and eat together, a significant ritual in these gatherings. The menu includes majadra, schnitzel and pitta with hummus, served on paper plates. During mealtime, the diners exchange experiences. There's no politics, just getting to know each other. Khaled, a Palestinian contractor who is building upscale houses near Tel Aviv, talks about his experiences on the Hajj—the pilgrimage to Mecca. Part of the idea at The Field is to create a place that is neither Jewish nor Palestinian, neither A nor B nor C, a place where the rituals of the encounters, the time these people spend together and the co-operative work they do, are the main thing. They do not sit here sketching outlines for a peace accord, but rather seek to establish a model for shared life. Most notably, no one here minimizes the significance of religion. On the contrary.

John Moyle, a hulking pastor from Virginia with a slight resemblance to the WWE wrestler John Cena, is the man responsible for The Field's emergence. He came to Israel a few years ago and held separate meetings with Jewish and Muslim clerics. "When I was here," he says, "I noticed the separation between the peoples. I studied the region's history and realized that, as the separation grows, so the conflict becomes uglier and more complicated. I wanted to find a way to stand in the middle and resist. Ever since then, I've been bringing people together, mostly religious people, from the two nations."

Moyle's words could be addressed to both the right and the center-left in Israel. Over the past decade, broad consent has emerged among the center-left parties that a walled state—in effect the largest Jewish ghetto in the world—is the solution we should aspire to, and that a Palestinian state should exist alongside it, borders to be determined. Other models for Jewish–Palestinian life in Israel—models that do not sanctify separation but rather support a collaborative, dynamic life—do not receive serious debate. The familiar "two states for two peoples" refrain, meant to "save Zionism and end the occupation," is practically the only line one hears from Israel's moderate factions.

At the same time that Moyle was setting up these joint meetings,

Ali began to formulate his idea for The Field and look for Jewish partners. After Rabbi Froman's death, Moyle brought Ali and his friends together with a few people from Gush Etzion, including Eliaz and Myron, and Hadassah Froman, the rabbi's widow, as well as some of his other relatives and disciples. Together, they conceived the model for The Field. The first thing they did was hold meetings between Jewish and Palestinian families, where the grown-ups talked and the kids played outside. They offered courses in Arabic and Hebrew, held youth events, and today they also maintain an organic farm together, growing produce and raising free-range chickens, farming the small vineyard and the orchard behind the barn.

One of Froman's students explains: "Isaac and Ishmael were brothers. That is the reality of the awake state, not the sleeping state. Our group here in The Field is small for now, but we may become large yet. We live terrible lives, everyone is afraid on the roads and contemplates death—how do we get out of that? The special thing about our group is that we are determined to learn how we can do this as one group."

"Jews and Palestinians are more antagonistic than ever in recent years," I observe, "and they are tired of one another. But you seem to be moving in the exact opposite direction."

Ali responds: "We really are asking: how can we teach Palestinian children not to hate, when the occupation soldiers are constantly in front of them? Who will remind Palestinians that the Jews were also created in God's image?"

"The key to the perception and the idea we are creating here is something we learned together from Rabbi Froman," Eliaz Cohen adds. "It's a matter of yielding versus control, and those are two opposing and contradictory concepts. Ali is teaching me what it means to yield. Can you imagine a settler who would give his land to a joint initiative with Palestinians, the way Ali gave his? Of course not. In Bnei Akiva[12], in the yeshivas, and in Gush Emunim, we grew up with the slogan 'The Land of Israel belongs to the People of Israel.' But that is exactly what we have to yield, to let go of. We have to stop the 'ownership' link. Rabbi Froman always said this is the land of peace, it is God's land. It takes enormous effort to release one's consciousness, to recognize that we are not the masters of the land or the owners of the land, but rather that we belong to the land. And here the slogan is flipped. 'The people of Israel belong to the Land of Israel,' and the Palestinians also belong to the Land of Israel, to Palestine."

"Many people reading what you say will think: this man sits there on occupied land, in a settlement in the heart of the Palestinian population—which, partly due to his presence, suffers daily violations of its rights—and talks about peace, love and brotherhood."

"That is an impertinent, leftist reaction that comes from a snobbish, patronizing, indulgent place, which for more than two decades has been lodging both peoples in the racist perception of us here and them there," Eliaz angrily responds. "It's a statement

12 The largest religious Zionist youth movement, with well over fifty thousand members in Israel.

that all sorts of visitors come here 'equipped with' but, the minute they see what we're doing here, what sort of partnership and mutual responsibility are being created in this place, their prejudices start evaporating and their confusion gives way to the beginning of a new consciousness, to a transformation like the one I mentioned. It happens to almost everyone who comes here, and it happens all the time to us, the activist-partners, on both sides."

Tariq, a young Palestinian, talks longingly about the phone book from before the First Intifada, which included both Jewish and Arab names. I've heard this nostalgic line on the West Bank before. "I remember that when I was a kid, in the eighties, my father's phone book was full of numbers. I'd see Yitzhak, Shlomo, Amnon. The people who worked with my father came to our home, we went to their weddings sometimes, in that era Jews and Arabs mingled. Then the leaderships decided to build a wall between the peoples, but that solution is dead now. The mingling between Jews and Arabs is the asset of this place. National and religious mingling. Our generation might be lost, but in another generation or two we will be able to live together."

Although the group is still small, a few significant initiatives have already sprung up. The members' determination and the realization that they really are creating a different kind of place were bolstered after the three Jewish boys were kidnapped not half a mile away from this spot. For years, Eliaz Cohen recounts, they'd been holding Jewish–Palestinian encounters but, any time there was a security event or blood was spilled, each side withdrew into its own fortress and everything stopped. This time, it

was a different story: immediately after the kidnapping they met
and decided to go ahead with the Palestinian–Jewish summer
camp they'd been planning, which was to culminate in a day at
the seaside together. Nitzanim Beach, which is not far from Gaza,
was declared too dangerous because of mortar bombs, so the kids
went to Sidna Ali Beach, just north of Tel Aviv. They also organized a joint Jewish–Muslim prayer for the kidnapped boys and,
after their bodies were found, the group paid a visit to the mourning tent of the Frankel family. Hundreds of people were there
when the delegation sat down with the Frankels, including ultra-
Orthodox Sephardic Jews, well-off Ashkenazi settlers, secular Tel
Avivis and other people from all over Israel. As they sat there,
Hadassah Froman overheard two Jews trying to force the scene
into their familiar value system: "But we do have a higher soul
than they do, don't we?" one of them whispered desperately.

Jamal, a Palestinian from Beit Ummar, says members of his
mosque attacked him because of his collaboration with the Jews.
But in the end, he says, the imam hugged him and told the con-
gregants: "He is a holy man who does what Mohammed did;
the Prophet also had Jewish friends." The night after their con-
dolence visit, they gathered at The Field and agreed to declare a
Jewish–Muslim fast—it was Ramadan and the Palestinians were
fasting anyway, but they decided to link the Muslim fast with
the Jewish fast of the Seventeenth of Tammuz. Against a backdrop of escalating violence and bloodshed, with the murder of
Mohammed Abu Khdeir and the war in Gaza, their initiative,
which they named "Choosing Life," gained momentum not only

in the area but among Palestinian and Jewish communities all over the country and the world.

In an interview with *Makor Rishon* shortly before his death, Rabbi Froman said: "For forty years I've been proposing this route. They called me a madman. Today they understand more…I studied Islam at Merkaz Ha'Rav, where I learned that religious people, who are the root of the problem, are also the root of the solution. Why am I such a supporter of interfaith peace? Because it's realistic. You can sweep the dust under the rug, but you can't sweep a tiger under the rug." I wonder about the validity of Froman's argument. It's interesting to note that those who cling to the two-state solution, and insist on pointing out how fantastical other ideas are, do not seem to question how many more years they can keep talking about that worn-out notion without sounding fantastical themselves. Will we still be discussing a Clinton-delineated two-state solution in 2045?

The Field was built on a foundation of religious peace as championed by Froman, on the notion that religious and spiritual experience must be given prominence. But Ali Abu Awwad and his Palestinian partners have added an important layer to this underpinning, one which privileged Jews from neighboring settlements were not familiar with: the language of non-violence. Ali invited these settlers into the Palestinians' non-violent struggle, which has been formulating its principles for the past several years and focuses on the Palestinians' rights in this arena, on the pilfering and the exploitation—a struggle by people whose central experience is the violation of their rights in all areas of life.

The constant sound of sirens reaches the barn from a distance, a reminder of the tensions between the real world of nearby Gush Etzion Junction—where people still get shot at, where soldiers man checkpoints and carry out arrests—and the reality this group is attempting to establish. After witnessing such great suffering in the region, it is tempting to believe in a place like The Field. It is almost possible to envision how this model, which at least for now is still fairly marginal, could sweep up Jews and Arabs enough to become a force in the region. One can imagine anything, and the need for sites of hope, after all the normalized scenes of cruelty, can blur one's judgement. The excessive sobriety which so many people here brag about can seem foolish, especially when it negates any chance of changing the future.

Most people at The Field insist that once the big agreements have failed, after all the talk and the speeches, reconciliation will begin in exactly these places: fields, groups, communities, small movements seeking to build a different life, lighthouses still hidden from view by the fog, but which in the future may light up the way for the masses.

* * *

After the murder of eighteen-month-old Ali Dawabsheh in an arson attack carried out by Jewish assailants, Yakov Nagen and Hadassah Froman organized a prayer at Gush Etzion to express their anguish. Ali Abu Awwad took part in the prayer.

"This is undoubtedly a welcome initiative, but the violence is only increasing," I suggest to Nagen. "How does one deal with the ideology of these people, the murderers and their supporters?"

"There is a saying that a little bit of light pushes out a lot of darkness. But the opposite is also true: a little darkness pushes out a lot of light," he responds. "These are small groups, not isolated individuals. They are people with an unruly, anti-establishment, anarchist doctrine, and they are contemptuous of authority. They're puncturing the tires of the Yesha Council. Tel Avivis may believe these people did what their rabbis told them to do, but you should know that that's nonsense, it's exactly the opposite: they disdain the rabbis, and view anyone who lives by the laws of the State of Israel as despicable collaborators. This attitude does exist and it must be dealt with firmly. But the question is what doctrine we hold up against it. This is the decisive question of our time: Is Israel one of the nations? And I say, yes! The Jewish people do have a role in the great story of humanity, but the Torah does not begin with Israel. It begins with all of humanity, the human race itself, and that is something I would like every person in Judea and Samaria, in Israel and in the world, to believe in."

9

Us Here, Them Here

Beit Jala, Bethlehem

I gaze out at the hundred-odd people waiting by the side of the road: thin young boys, guys in their twenties, bearded middle-aged men. Some stand on the curb expectantly, others lean on the fence behind, smoke cigarettes under a tree, or sit on the sidewalk drinking coffee. One man tears pieces off a loaf of bread and hands them out to his friends. There is little talk, and the rest of the street is empty. It's still dark at 6.20 a.m., with a cool breeze and the occasional drizzle. The men huddle in their coats or crowd under the grocery store's awning. Cars, pick-up trucks and buses pull up regularly, and small groups of men get on. They are headed to jobs in Israel, mostly around Jerusalem. The group dwindles. Not everyone will find work today; some will go home.

We drive through the Palestinian village of Beit Jala and park outside the Everest Hotel, where we've come for a "Two States One Homeland" meeting. The hotel balcony looks out onto a rocky, mountainous landscape, a military base and "Tunnel Road"—a portion of Highway 60 that connects Gush Etzion and Hebron with Jerusalem, bypassing the west side of Bethlehem. The Israelis among us remember shootings on that road during the Second Intifada, an experience not easily forgotten, much like the shots fired on the predominantly Jewish neighborhood of Gilo in Jerusalem. It's mid-December, but the long tables with red tablecloths in the hotel's ill-lit dining room are deserted. Perhaps the tourists will come next week, closer to Christmas. Many of Beit Jala's Christian residents have left over the past couple of decades. On a recent visit to Mexico, I met a young website designer whose family had moved to Mexico City from Beit Jala in 1987, at the beginning of the First Intifada. He was born in Mexico and had never been to Beit Jala, but one day he planned "to go home to visit." His aunts and uncles are scattered all over the world: Beit Jala, Ramallah, Saudi Arabia, Qatar, the United States, Chile.

About twenty people are waiting in the icy conference room,

including a few familiar faces: Munir Abushi, Awni al-Mashni and Muhammad al-Beiruti, whom we've met frequently at their Ramallah offices. We are friendly at this point and, as happens in every group, we've cultivated our own social dynamics, our own cliques. I am especially fond of al-Beiruti and try to get a seat next to him. He is smart, knowledgeable about the conflict's history, and not averse to poking fun at the long-winded orations delivered by some other members. We've already agreed that a few people in the group could do with a "pathos vaccination." The room is furnished with nothing but a large table and chairs, and the walls are bare. It's a familiar setting: we held our inaugural gathering here two years ago. "Two States One Homeland" was originally conceived by al-Mashni and the Israeli journalist Meron Rapoport about three years ago. At the time, al-Mashni advocated a single state for everyone (as far as he was concerned, it could be called Israel), where Palestinians would have equal rights and full freedom of movement and would even serve in the army, and to which refugees would be allowed to gradually return. Rapoport did not believe this idea could possibly gain political traction in Israel, and favored the concept of two states within a shared space. They worked together to formulate a model they viewed as an acceptable midway point between the one-state concept and the familiar 1990s two-state solution. The initiative has evolved since then, on both the Israeli and the Palestinian sides. Some of our meetings have ended in discord, like one in this hotel a year ago, when it seemed we would never reach a resolution about the right of return; others have concluded with elation, as when we unanimously approved the final paper outlining the initiative's principles. We have met during times of military operations and bloodshed, when everything seemed to be falling apart around us, but we've had days when we truly believed our proposal offers a just and creative solution and, more importantly, a viable one, to the conflict's chief issues. Some very enthusiastic participants, on both sides, have dropped out, whether for personal reasons or because they could not accept some of our solutions; new people, though, have joined along the way.

A few months and one Gaza war have passed since we met with the PLO's Muhammad al-Madani, and meanwhile we've begun a controlled exposure of the initiative to thousands of people on both sides, mostly through salons held in the homes of Israelis and Palestinians. It has been a struggle to find our place among the classic two-state believers and the one-state advocates, who are multiplying rapidly, especially among West Bank Palestinians and Israeli-Palestinian citizens. We now face a new challenge: we've had lengthy debates about the right time to go public, and there have always seemed to be reasons to wait, whether it was John Kerry's negotiations, the 2014 Gaza war or the upcoming elections in Israel. But impatience has been mounting, and we all feel ready. We believe our plan is a good one, we can all see the massive despair and we know that in this part of the world there is no such thing as "the right time." So we've decided it's time to "come out," regardless of any political events in the background. Today we will discuss the publicity plans and figure out how to proceed without a political mechanism, without funds, without the support of parties or big movements. We knew from the beginning that we did not want to become yet another international initiative with lots of European money and outmoded principles. Instead, we've worked to nurture a slowly simmering Palestinian–Israeli grassroots movement.

Each participant is asked to name the most significant aspect of the initiative in their view—the one thing we think should be underscored in public presentations. The official minutes are being recorded by Buran Saadi, who teaches at the Palestine College for Police Sciences in Jericho, but I notice four other people taking notes. The best proposal comes from Eliaz Cohen, the poet from Gush Etzion, who suggests, "Us here, them here," a clever reversal of the familiar "Us here, them there" slogan. His idea is met with enthusiasm on both sides, because after all one of our central tenets is our objection to the separation between the peoples, which most of us believe is no longer attainable anyway. Al-Beiruti offers his own motto: "Jews and Palestinians: let's make one state like in Europe, and move to Paris together." Someone else offers: "The nineties are over; here's a peace plan that can be implemented immediately."

The discussion moves to the Israeli elections due to be held in March 2015. One of the Palestinians says that a week ago the Palestinian president Abu Mazen hosted a few dozen Israeli-Palestinian businessmen and community leaders, and urged them to run as a joint party. ("This is a scoop!" one Israeli whispers to me. "Abu Mazen is intervening directly in the Israeli elections.") But Munir Abushi argues that Israeli Arabs are better off integrating within parties across the spectrum, including Labor, Likud and Meretz, which will afford them greater influence on the political system. Tactically, he is clearly right.

Seated next to me is a newcomer, a young man from Isawiya, who is the only person here dressed in a suit and tie. He tells me that, when he was doing his MA in Oman, he organized a Palestinian student group. The Israeli Palestinians, he says, were adamant about underscoring their differences from the rest of the group. He is writing his doctoral dissertation now. His topic? "Between Extinction and Disappearance: Stories of Christian Arabs in Palestine."

Khaled, the Hebronite we met earlier, offers his position: "In 1975, I was in prison in Be'er Sheva with the guys here, al-Beiruti and the others. All day long we read books and talked about politics and life. I ended up reading Theodor Herzl, and I learned that he had an idea for a common society where governance would be divided between Arabs and Jews. I think the two-state idea is a clear outcome of Zionism. In practice, we've been living in a single state for decades, and the only solution is one state for all residents. Total equality leads to total justice, and a distribution of the burden."

Munir brings up the phone-book anecdote again: "Thirty years ago everyone had a phone book with Jewish and Arab names. Ever since the arrival of the peace idea, with the Oslo accords and the separation, there are no Arabs in the Jews' phone books and vice versa."

Khaled and Munir, though critical of the Oslo Accords, do

make favorable mention of Yitzhak Rabin, "may he rest in peace," demonstrating once again that the only people who still talk about Rabin are the Palestinians. "There's something you have to understand," says Khaled. "The Palestinians are prepared to accept one state, or two states, just as long as the occupation ends. You don't understand the Palestinians' daily life. It's harsher than any of the plans or initiatives. We want our daily existence to change, we want freedom of movement, and any proposal that changes the situation is good. Your Israelis' debate is more abstract, always focused on the principles of a final agreement, because you don't feel the occupation except once in a while when there's a terrorist attack." Then he adds: "I think the slogan for the Israelis should be: 'Herzl willed it.'"

During our break, the young man from Isawiya, who wants to remain anonymous, tells me he can't find a job. He got married recently, and he and his wife still live with his parents. He's been sending his resume out to all sorts of organizations in Jerusalem and Tel Aviv, but he hasn't even been interviewed. He's consider-ing moving to Ramallah or Jordan. He likes Jerusalem, but he didn't spend all those years studying in London, Oman and Israel to waste his time at an office job or sit at home unemployed. He says Khaled's criticism of the Oslo Accords is not unfounded: all the Fatah men in the room, including Khaled, had pinned a lot of hopes on Oslo, and in retrospect they believe it was largely an Israeli fraud. His father, he says, always viewed Oslo as a disas-ter. "Oslo was where they basically invented Area C in the West Bank, which includes all the settlements and lots of other lands, which they removed from the Palestinian Authority's jurisdiction. In return for gaining control over a few Palestinian cities, the Tunis leadership accepted the existence of the settlements. From that moment on, the PA couldn't even file a court appeal against Israel's demands to set up or expand settlements in Area C. The Palestinians effectively agreed to the settlements, and the settlements grew a lot as a result of that, and then Israel demanded to annex more land in the final accord."

His view of things reminds me of Raja Shehadeh's position. I think of how, in the nineties, we were all convinced that the Oslo Accords would lead to real peace. We couldn't understand Palestinians, such as Edward Said or Haidar Abdel-Shafi (who headed the Palestinian delegation to the Madrid talks in 1991), who opposed Oslo and saw it as a historic mistake. In hindsight, of course, this young man's account seems accurate, but one could so easily imagine how a final agreement could have been reached at Camp David fifteen years ago, or if Prime Minister Rabin hadn't been assassinated, in which case the Oslo Accords might have gone down in history as a brilliant concept which ultimately led to a resolution of this thorny conflict. But the history of the past two decades bolsters the position of those Palestinians who remained pessimistic in 1993.

After our break, Awni al-Mashni, who gets impatient when the speeches draw on and we get sidetracked by political gossip, says that Palestinians are generally suspicious of Israeli initiatives like the Geneva and Oslo accords. As he sees it, the pattern is that Israel turns up with a proposal, pressures the Palestinians to accept it, then a month later reneges on some of the principles, and demands that the Palestinians still acquiesce. The Palestinians have seen this strategy one too many times, and there is no chance they will support our initiative until Israeli constituents commit to it. One of the Israelis says that will be very difficult, because it's actually the Israelis who will want to be convinced that there is a Palestinian partner. The ideas we are proposing are far-reaching for Israeli Jews, particularly free transit between the two states and the right of every citizen in one state to be a resident of the other. Although we are not talking about granting citizenship, this issue will still provoke fears among Jews that they are destined to live in an Arab state. It's clear to us all that acceptance of the initiative by Israelis will require a profound conceptual revolution: an abandonment of the separation principle in favor of a pursuit of shared life in all areas. That day is still far away.

The meeting ends with a series of decisions about publicity events, and we set up a joint co-ordinating committee. The main idea is to organize two gatherings, one in Tel Aviv and one in Ramallah, where the initiative will be revealed. Most participants hurry home when we're done, but a handful of us stay on for lunch at the hotel. We fill one table in the spacious dining room; all the others are empty. It's cold here, and we eat with our coats on. Waiters pile our table with dishes of institutional food—tasteless rice and chicken, and various salads. Both the Palestinians and the Israelis complain about how expensive the food is (100 shekels a head) and how bad.

I sit with Munir, al-Beiruti, Khaled and a real estate developer from Ramallah named Abu Ghosh, another of their prison-mates from Be'er Sheva, who used his time there to learn French. I make another attempt to find out why they were arrested, but I get the familiar vague replies. "Number one!" Munir reminds me; he finds an opportunity at every meeting to point out that he was Israel's most wanted man. "At least for a while," al-Beiruti adds, and everyone laughs. After lunch, a few of us decide to drive to nearby Bethlehem. I lived in Jerusalem after the Oslo Accords and my friends and I used to sometimes drive to Bethlehem to see the Church of the Nativity, eat at local restaurants, wander around the market and drive the city roads. We were in our late teens, and we loved the idea that Bethlehem was so accessible, that we could just get in our car and travel around the PA's state and see Palestinian policemen and cars with green license plates. But, apart from one hasty visit, I haven't seen Bethlehem in fifteen years.

The clouds have cleared, and the sun shines down on the Church of the Nativity when we stop outside. A group of young girls in fancy white dresses snap pictures of themselves, then look at the screen together and giggle. Tourists, peddlers and curious onlookers, many dressed in their finest clothes, mingle in the square. A week from now, the main Christmas mass will be held here. Before the State of Israel was founded, Christians were the overwhelming majority in Bethlehem, constituting seven out of eight households. Official numbers show they are only about forty percent of the city's population today, although the real figure is widely believed to be even lower. I meet a Christian Arab family from Kfar Kanna, in the Galilee, who proudly explain that Jesus began his journey in their village, where he turned water into wine. Kfar Kanna was once bigger than Nazareth, they tell me nostalgically, but today it's small. Then they talk about the Pope, who visited here last May and gave a speech outside the church, right at this spot: What a wonderful day that was! There was a big stage set up, and giant screens everywhere with the caption "Friend." There were Vatican and PA flags flying everywhere, and the crowd was so excited, and then the Pope arrived.

They are surprised to learn that I was here that day too. "Do you remember," I ask, "how in the middle of the speech we suddenly heard the *muezzin* from the nearby mosque, and the Pope's speech was interrupted, and there was a sort of stunned silence in the square? But then the Pope resumed speaking, with the *muezzin*'s voice still audible, and the crowd got angry and whistled and booed and clapped, and everyone wondered if the Muslims were deliberately disrupting the Pope's visit?"

"No, we don't remember," they answer coolly. "Well, maybe dimly." They walk away, irritated.

We drive to a restaurant I used to know well. Unlike in Beit Jala, the streets here are full of tourists and the city center is bustling. As we get closer to the restaurant, which I remember was located on the outskirts of town, maybe five minutes from the church, I suddenly realize we're heading straight into the separation wall. I know this road well from the nineties, but now it's truncated by the wall, pieces of which seem to glare back from every direction, closing in on us. The restaurant has vanished, but then I understand it's on the other side of the wall, probably right up against the gates, which are shut now: it is no longer in Bethlehem.

We stop the car at the wall and sit silently gazing out. It's so tempting to view all the laws and customs we have evolved over the years of occupation as extra baggage of sorts, which we will one day be able to shed and become different people in doing so. This fantasy is prevalent among certain circles in Israel, but at some point we have to realize—and probably did a long time ago, if we're being honest—that our laws and customs *are* us.

10

Where Are the Arabs Here, Anyway?

The Itamar Outposts and Yanun

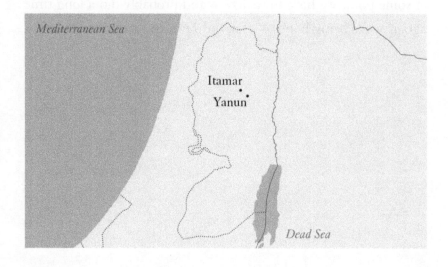

On the way out of Tel Aviv, huge campaign posters for the center-left parties (Zionist Union, Meretz, Yesh Atid) are plastered on every high-rise and billboard. Everywhere I look, I encounter the wrinkled visage of Zionist Union leader Yitzhak Herzog, looking a bit like a farmer who fell asleep under the midday sun. The signs, the faces and the slogans accost us with their loud colors, and for a moment the elections—still too close to call in the polls—seem genuinely to hold the power to bring change. But as we make our way along Highway 5 toward Ariel, the signs disappear along with the traffic. On this road we see fewer election posters than on any other in Israel. At most the occasional picture of a candidate from Ha'Bayit Ha'Yehudi is stuck to a rock on the side of the road. It's Friday; the elections are in four days.

The traffic light at the turn-off to the settlement of Immanuel is the last one on the highway. From here on it's quieter, with almost no traffic or honking, and a landscape of olive trees, lawns and other greenery, with the occasional cluster of houses and a mosque. At Ariel Intersection there are lots of ads for the Yachad party and its star, Baruch Marzel (the self-professed right-hand man of the assassinated rabbi Meir Kahane and now a vocal champion of his agenda), lots of "Only Netanyahu" signs, but no canvassers or much excitement of any kind. Politics tend to proceed at a lazy pace, occasionally punctuated by a frenzy. Two months ago we were traveling this same area during the heady days of Ha'Bayit Ha'Yehudi's surge in the polls, when everyone was jumping on that bandwagon. But now the party is struggling to stay in the double-digits, with Likud nipping at it from one side and Yachad from the other, capitalizing on the disillusionment with Naftali Bennett among the Nationalist-Orthodox camp. It's tempting to correlate the lack of election fever around here with Ha'Bayit Ha'Yehudi's drop in the polls, but the fact is that these streets were just as sleepy back then; truth be told, it's hard to find much enthusiasm for politics anywhere these days.

The road curves ahead and opens onto a swath of dark green hills. At Tapuach Junction, a lively central artery in the West Bank, Palestinians and Jews sit at a falafel restaurant and shop at the produce store across the street. This junction is one of the area's primary meeting (and at times, friction) points between Palestinians and Jews. We take the recently upgraded road to Tapuach, pass a sign declaring "Phase 1 is sold out!" and pull up next to a white four-wheel drive.

Tirael Cohen steps out of the vehicle wearing faded jeans, a white T-shirt and sunglasses, with long hair that waves in the wind. I ask her about the yawning atmosphere—where's the election excitement? "The activist right doesn't exist anymore," she asserts. "Before the disengagement there were public leaders, but now it's less noticeable." We drive through Huwara with Tirael, who describes it as a hostile village. When I express skepticism, she says that in 2014, during Operation Protective Edge, she was driving this road with her dog one day when she heard a loud noise. When she got to Tapuach Junction and stopped, she saw a blackened spot on her engine hood and realized a Molotov cocktail had just missed her.

Tirael was born twenty-two years ago to French immigrant parents in Modi'in, a booming city located partly over the Green Line, halfway between Jerusalem and Tel Aviv. Her mother has a PhD in biology and her father works in the IT field, and for a while they lived in San Francisco, a time Tirael remembers as "a very alienating experience." But as a teenage child of a middle-class Mizrahi religious family in Modi'in, something strange happened to her: she fell in love with the Shomron.

With a broad grin that belies the pathos in her voice, she recalls: "The land spoke to me, or something like that. I suddenly understood that this belongs to me, that my Jewish soul is connected to this place." She came to the Shomron for the first time at the age of fourteen, after the 2005 disengagement from Gaza, when many settlers were left feeling that their entire vision had been destroyed and the Israeli government could no longer be trusted, and in some cases even experienced a profound crisis of faith. Tirael joined up with a group of activists who had not accepted Israel's withdrawal and were determined to resettle the area and fight against any further evacuations. The first outpost she was involved in was called Reches Ramat Migron, near the original Migron outpost, which, with a population of fifty households, was the largest in the West Bank. The offshoot was set up in protest after Migron's residents reached an agreement with the government to leave voluntarily by the end of 2015. (Migron did not last that long: it was forcefully evacuated in 2012 on orders from the Supreme Court, which found the agreement illegal.)

Tirael was part of a group of young teenaged girls who were staunchly Zionist and fueled with determination to settle the land all the more forcefully after the disengagement. She describes life on the outpost as a victory of the spirit over the body, and says the girls ran the show while the boys worked for them. They built huts from a type of particle board. Sometimes they were evacuated or arrested, but they always went back.

"What did your parents think about their little girl, a straight-A student, living on an illegal outpost in the Shomron?"

As it turns out, her parents loved the idea. They knew they had raised an ardent Zionist. "A classic, boring Zionist," as Tirael puts it. She is quick to point out that there was "a lot of modesty" at the outpost. Rumors about relationships between the teenagers, and about recreational drugs, flew around provincial Shomron, and in response the girls kept an even greater distance from the boys. They treated the settlement enterprise with the utmost gravity. She still has notebooks with minutes from their meetings, where they debated such issues as "The Jews: where to?" as well as who was on cleaning duty. "I was a hilltop girl par excellence," she laughs, "but the hilltop youth is a bit of a legend. We girls studied, took our matriculation exams, volunteered. The boys were a different story maybe." After a few years the place was taken over by settlers whom Tirael found too religious. She left behind her youthful outpost, but not the ideas she had developed there. Sometimes you have to take a deep breath and make a new approach from a different angle.

We drive through Itamar, which is almost completely devoid of election signs, and continue on a narrow road with the Shomron's breathtaking landscape ahead. This road connects the seven outposts scattered around the hills with their "mother settlement" of Itamar. "Most of the population here is socio-economically tough," Tirael explains. "There's a hilltop of Breslavs here, and that's Yanuach Hill, where only veteran Russian immigrants live." We stop next to several large chicken coops belonging to the outpost Gvaot Olam, where Avri Ran, a well-known outpost activist, farms organic eggs and makes cheese. Tirael also mentions the cheese made at another outpost, Eretz U'Meloah Farm. Then we look out onto Hill 851, where a former pilot built a small airfield. It's hard to encompass all the outposts with their myriad stories, inhabitants and exploits. "When everything's forbidden, everything's allowed," Tirael explains. "The minute you have a sweeping prohibition against something, an underground culture springs up with its own laws. The law does not recognize the hilltops."

"But the hilltops get assistance, don't they? Who paved this road? And the power here—is it from the sun?"

"The settlement of Itamar spurns the hilltops, it doesn't really want them," she insists. "These are the places that even Amana and all the other institutions ignore. When it snowed, we had no power for a month."

"Okay," I concede. "You can have the last word."

We stand at a lookout point observing the endless, vivid horizon. Beneath us are the houses of Nablus, and we can see all three of the region's large bodies of water: the Dead Sea on the right, Lake Tiberias in the middle and the Mediterranean on the left. Sometimes the brightly colored scenery looks artificial, like a movie set from a Western. The silence is suddenly pierced by a screeching of brakes, and a group of older Americans get out of a car. They are dressed expensively, with flashy rings and gold chains, and they gather around to listen to their tour guide's tales about Abraham's adventures on this very spot. They stand looking at him wide-eyed, occasionally sighing with deep reverence.

I naively assume this is an ordinary tourists' excursion, but it turns out I have completely missed the point. After the tour guide greets Tirael, who answers coolly, I learn that this place is known as "donation hilltop." Potential donors, usually Evangelicals, are brought here to witness the biblical rocky terrain where Abraham and Isaac walked, and are then prodded to make a contribution. The tour guide is actually the director of a non-profit in Itamar. "I asked him to give money to our community," Tirael hisses, "but I guess he's not into it." So it turns out that, just like in Tel Aviv, on this desolate hilltop in the Shomron, among the most isolated of outposts, you will always find members of the not-for-profit sector competing over donors and resources.

We drive to Hill 777, the last outpost on the range, where Tirael Cohen began her social-activism career. No longer the rebellious hilltop youth, she now has a reputation as an energetic activist in the settlements and the outposts. She is also earning her BA in communications at Tel Aviv University, on a full merit-based scholarship. Most of her fellow students vote for left-wing parties. "I would get on my moped at five in the morning and drive this road, past wild boars and birds, to the university." She waxes poetic, but quickly recognizes the dubious look on my face. "I swear, on a moped! In winter I'd get there with muddy boots, and in my screenwriting class I'd tell them about the donkey that wouldn't get off the road. Everyone there looked at me like I was some exotic creature. I was living in two different worlds."

This is an accurate description of Tirael's existence, and she is fluent in both languages: the settlers' vernacular of land and

Jewish soul, and the political jargon of human rights and social activism that prevails in Tel Aviv. "I'm not interested in people who are all talk. If you believe in something—on the left, too—then go out to the streets, demonstrate. If Tel Aviv is too expensive for you, move to Be'er Sheva. Have some connection between your worldview and your life. This is what I believe and this is my life: I am exactly the person I dreamed of being, I'm fulfilling my dreams. Can your friends say the same thing about themselves?"

Hill 777 is perched atop a winding road at the edge of the ridge, some seven miles from Itamar, and is surrounded by greenery, olive trees and wheat fields. Before reaching the houses, I stop at a small playground whose bright colors stand out against the drab buildings. To the left of the road, behind a recycling station, are two large stone houses with red-tiled roofs in the typical settlement style. Opposite them is a huddle of shacks and dark trailers made of old wooden beams. A few cars are parked outside the shacks, and dogs run around the laundry lines, barking. I spot a few people around: a young couple walks serenely down the road, a boy plays with a rifle in the yard. There are about fifteen homes here.

"What do people here do for a living?" I ask Tirael.

"Some of them farm. There are vineyards nearby." Actual vineyards? "Yes, vineyards, and there are olive groves too. One of the residents owns a small winery, another is a cosmetician in Itamar, some work outside the community, in Tel Aviv and elsewhere. In the shack opposite us there's a family that was evacuated from Gush Katif." The population she describes is a far cry from the typical hilltop youth one expects to find in this sort of remote outpost.

We reach Tirael's first project, a student village she founded a few years ago. It resides in the outpost's largest structure, one of the big stone houses, and includes a spacious living room, kitchen, nine bedrooms and a yard. There are currently a dozen female students living here, but a few have gone home for Shabbat. We are greeted by two young women cooking breakfast in the kitchen. They study criminology and social science at Beit Berl College, near Tel Aviv.

I ask Tirael how she ended up at this outpost.

"This community was started by people from Hosen Yehudi Le'Yisrael.[13] A few years after moving here, they grew tired of it and slowly abandoned the site, until there was only one family left. A kibbutznik from Ein Ha'Natziv who fell in love with this place built the house we're in now, but he abandoned it. At that time I was living in Ofra, and I kept thinking about how I could be an activist after my experience at Migron. I came up with this model of student villages in disadvantaged communities, where the students would volunteer in the community and lift it up. I started talking with the Shomron Regional Council and I found this empty house. To my surprise, I had no trouble recruiting students. We came here and asked people how we could help. We

---

13 "Jewish Strength for Israel," a small movement made up of secular and religious Israelis, ranging from IT workers to former kibbutz members.

started a Hebrew language program on the Russians' hilltop and three daycare centers."

"How did they welcome you on the hilltops?"

"It wasn't easy. The students who come here are from all over Israel, not from the Shomron. So at first they were suspicious, until they got used to us and realized we were helping them. Over time I discovered that we have crazy community power; I mean, nobody believed the students would survive here."

For a long time now, the settlement enterprise has not been the exclusive purview of religious Ashkenazis following their rabbis, but has attracted people from all strata of Israeli society: Mizrahis, Russians, secular, traditional. In a 2009 study, Rivi Gillis found that the division is roughly thirty-six percent Ashkenazis, thirty percent Mizrahis, and thirty-four percent native Israelis of indeterminate ethnicity. Most of the women in the student house are from the Central Region. Yaffit, from Kfar Shalem, a low-income neighborhood in south Tel Aviv, is studying at Ariel University.

"How did you end up here?" I ask her.

"They were handing out fliers on campus. I love the Shomron, and when I came here the first time and saw the amazing views from the window, I said: This will be my home."

"Do your parents know where you live?"

"My mother doesn't know what the Shomron is and she's not excited about it. I come from a national-religious home, but then I became secular, and now I'm becoming religious again."

"What are your duties here?"

"I volunteer at the daycare center. Working with the children, and living here with the girls, far away from all the noise, is wonderful in my view."

"How much rent do you pay?"

"Two hundred and fifty shekels a month." (For comparison's sake, one would be hard-pressed to rent a room in Tel Aviv for less than 1,500 shekels.)

A student from Ramla, an impoverished city in central Israel, tells us: "The girls who live here did not arrive by accident. I always wanted to settle the land, I dreamed of living with my husband in a trailer or a tent. Everyone in my family supports Greater Israel, but I'm the only one who moved to a settlement."

I go outside and stand in the yard with two of the students. It's warm here, and everything around us is gray-green. They point to a house on a desolate patch just over a mile away, toward the Jordan Valley. "There's another family living there," they crow. "Wonderful people. They live on a strategic point; the big goal is to get Jewish continuity from here to the Jordan Valley."

"That does seem a little far," I point out.

"Step by step, it'll happen," one of the women replies. "And once there is continuity, everyone will be able to talk until the Messiah comes, but what matters are the facts."

I think about the settlers' frequent claim that in the West Bank ties between Jews and Arabs are closer than inside the Green Line. I ask these women: "Do you run into Arabs from the surrounding villages? Is there any contact?"

My question surprises them. "There is no contact with the

local Arabs. Maybe people who work in agriculture have slightly more contact with them."

When Tirael joins us, I repeat the students' vision of Jewish continuity all the way to the Jordan Valley. "What rights," I ask her, "do the Palestinians who live here have?"

"Humanity is an important thing, there are other human beings living here. I'm working within my world, I encounter the hardships of Jews who live here because it's a geographical periphery and lots—"

I interrupt her. "We've already talked about that. I asked about the Palestinians' rights."

"The only meeting point I know of is on the roads, which is a charged and not always pleasant encounter, because every accident can turn into a nationalist affair. But the answer is simple: I believe in the Jewish people's right to the land. I need to know which territory belongs to me. I'm far from understanding the Palestinian side, and I don't pretend to analyze their aspirations. And the truth is that I don't come up against that question. I bring students here, or to Rimonim, and they always seem surprised. 'Where are the Arabs here, anyway?' they ask."

Indeed, where are they?

* * *

We're on yet another narrow, winding road full of craters and mounds. All around us is desolate silence, except a few olive trees and birds. Another bend and another incline and the road seems to be leading nowhere. Finally we stop outside a stone house. An old car is parked outside, there is junk scattered around, and two donkeys are passed out in the heat next to a small tree that offers little shade. There is no one around, and I get the feeling I've reached a place that no longer exists, like so many other abandoned Palestinian villages marked only by a few surviving stone houses.

The tiny West Bank village of Khirbet Yanun a'Takhta is home to a few dozen people and is located in Area B, meaning it is under Israeli security control but Palestinian civil authority. Brambles and twigs snap under my feet as I walk over the dry earth. A few structures, scattered at the end of the hilltops surrounding us some distance away, mark the outline of the Itamar Ridge outposts. I can just make out one of Hill 777's houses.

I climb up a staircase sheltered by fruit trees and sit down in the outdoor living room, a sort of parlor. The walls are bare, and the room is furnished with a few plaid couches topped with gold-threaded cushions, and a wooden table covered by a white tablecloth. The homeowners have clearly put a lot of effort into disguising their poverty with this living room. The head of the household is a thin, bearded man in his fifties with a deeply wrinkled face. He apologizes for not being able to offer us water, due to Ramadan. He speaks softly, and is clearly a shy man. I can hear the voices of his wife and children from behind the door. He prefers not to give his name. When I ask why, he says he's been in trouble with the army more than once.

The village of Yanun has been here for years, "Even from before the Ottomans," as my host explains, "and it survived all the various occupiers." His grandparents moved here because they needed grazing land for their sheep and goats, and there was also a bounteous wellspring nearby. Yanun's villagers have always made a living from farming, growing olive trees, tobacco, hazelnuts, almonds and wheat. After Israel occupied the land in 1967, it built a military base nearby, but the soldiers didn't get in the way of the villagers' work. Sometimes the farmers would inform the soldiers about their farming schedules so that they wouldn't do military exercises at inconvenient times. In the mid-1980s, the settlement of Itamar was built to the west of Yanun. At first it was just one house in a fenced-off plot, and they didn't worry about it too much. Then more and more houses went up. My host says that Itamar's original borders included unfarmed lands owned by Arabs who were living elsewhere. But after a while the settlement began the typical creep, expanding and sloping down into the plains, taking over lands farmed by residents of Aqraba and Awarta (much larger communities), which the settlers used mostly for their own animals to graze. Next came the outposts of Itamar Ridge, built mostly starting in the late nineties: Gvaot Olam, Yanuach, Hill 777, Alumot and others. As the settlement sent out more and more tentacles and took over more and more land, the Palestinian farmers suffered increasingly frequent humiliations, curses and sometimes beatings when they came to work their lands. My host tells me that the settlers once grabbed a shepherd from Aqraba and poisoned his whole flock. At the beginning of 2014, local settlers cut down about sixty olive trees owned by Yanun villagers.

I stare at video images of the ancient trees with their trunks cut down, some sliced in half, with the severed roots entangled between the parts. There is nothing I can say, and the words around me blur into a meaningless hum. I am overwhelmed by all the sights of this past year on the West Bank, and they flicker together at the forefront of my consciousness until I can no longer see a thing.

Over time, the restrictions imposed by the army on the farmers' access to their lands grew more stringent. During the Second Intifada the Palestinians became increasingly fearful and virtually stopped farming; they certainly lacked their previous dedication.

"I have olive groves around the outposts," my host continues, "so if I have to plow, they give me two days when the army is supposed to protect me. Tending to the olive trees has become a twice-yearly affair: after the rains they let us plow, and once a year they let us harvest. The rest of the time I'm not allowed to go to my land."

"How often did you used to visit your groves before the outposts were built?"

"Every day or two." He smiles bitterly. "I used to go and remove stones, weed, pull up thistles. I plowed a few times a year—not just once. It's very important for the crop. Last year they gave us five to seven days for the harvest. If someone wanted more time they got it, but the olives were in such bad condition that I didn't need more time." He used to produce fifty gallons of olive oil a year, but his recent output is about twenty gallons, most of which is used by his family, not sold. He's walked over to his land without permission several times, but when the settlers see him, they threaten him and tell him to go back home immediately. Sometimes the army forces him back. He says many Palestinians here used to have agricultural lands in the Jordan Valley, but after Itamar expanded it effectively swallowed up the access route from the villages to the valley, and the Palestinians can no longer use it. The only other path is longer and goes through Aqraba, and eventually the farmers just gave up their lands.

In the past, Palestinians filed repeated complaints with the army about being denied access to their lands, as well as about settlers' violence. My host lodged complaints too, but they weren't genuinely addressed, no one was punished, and usually the complaints only harmed whoever filed them and wasted their time, sometimes even leading to settler recrimination. So he stopped complaining. And because it's so hard to make a living from farming now, many people in Yanun have started working elsewhere. My host often enters Israel illegally to work for Israeli-Arab farmers in the Galilee. He pays five hundred shekels to smugglers who get him into Israel, which is a lot of money for him, but the average pay for farming in the PA is twenty-five hundred shekels a month, while in Israel he can make up to four or five thousand shekels.

As we are about to leave, he casually informs me that his son is under arrest in Tiberias, where he was caught yet again trying to cross the wall to the Israeli side. If you get caught the first time, they kick you back to the checkpoint, but the second time they press charges. I wonder how this man could have sat here chatting with us as though he had all the time in the world, while his son was in jail. Seeming to sense my question, he says there's nothing he can really do now.

About a mile uphill from his house lies Upper Yanun, a tiny part of the village with a clear view of the surrounding outposts: Gvaot Olam above us, Hill 777 across the way. I sit under a large fig tree with the elderly, bald man who owns this land, and who also does not want to give his name. "My father was the first Palestinian who was attacked by settlers from Itamar. He was working his land, and the settlers came and almost beat him to death with sticks and stones. He lost an eye," he recounts serenely. The heat is very harsh on this summer day, but it's surprisingly cool under the tree. "The settler who beat him built a house on Itamar with a fence around it, and then the army paved roads for them, the bulldozers graded land for them, they put down trailers, built houses, and started taking over more and more land."

I ask if he's afraid to stay here.

"They attack us all the time. In 2002 we all fled, we left our homes and moved to the area around Aqraba because we couldn't take it anymore, we were afraid for the kids. But I came back after three days. I have nothing except this place. Some people didn't come back, that's also why there's hardly anyone left here."

I walk around his home on an unpaved floor that resembles the damp, smooth ground of a cave. The house is poorly lit and has no refrigerator, barely any furniture, no toilet, and no running water. His children move around the rooms silently. In both parts of the village, the only creatures who make any loud sounds or lively moves are the cats. He points to a fence some distance away, surrounded by tall green grass and mossy rocks: this fence now separates him from most of his lands. He is not allowed to cross it or even get near it. He tells me about a friend from Nablus who owned lands near the outposts; the state confiscated them and now the settlers have vineyards there.

Like all the residents of Yanun, this man makes a minimal living from olives, wheat, sheep and goats—he keeps a flock in a cave behind the house. His sons help out with the farming and sometimes work construction on the West Bank. He is very proud of his youngest daughter, a student in Jerusalem, but he says that it will be a disaster if his two sons want to go to university too, because he can't support that many students. They won't come back here anyway: young people don't stay, they always move to Nablus or Aqraba, and they talk of emigrating to wherever they can. A few years from now there may no longer be a village here. I recall another passage from Raja Shehadeh's *Palestine Walks*, about a man named Abu Amin, a stonemason who loved the hills around Ramallah and built a house there, and was proud of it, and never left the area he'd been born in. Of his seven children and their forty offspring, not even one stayed on.

In 2004, Limor Yehuda, an attorney with the Association for Civil Rights in Israel, filed a Supreme Court petition on behalf of Palestinians from Yanun, Inbus and Burin, villages near the Itamar Ridge settlements of Yitzhar and Bracha. She recounts:

"The IDF began preventing Palestinian farmers from the villages near the settlements, including the outposts on the hilltops east of Itamar, from working their lands. In 2004, they significantly expanded the range of lands where entrance was prohibited, and it reached several dozen acres. The army made an interesting claim: they argued they were preventing the Palestinians from farming their lands for their own good, to protect them from harassment by the hilltop settlers, who had a history of attacks and provocations. In other words, instead of protecting the Palestinian farmers, the IDF decided to solve the problem by prohibiting them from accessing their lands. In the first hearing, before judges Beinisch, Rivlin and Jubran, the state attorney naturally defended the IDF's position, but she added another argument: the prohibition was also intended to protect the settlements."

In her attempt to justify this second argument, the state attorney began reading out an IDF report but, instead of describing acts of sabotage on the settlements, she recited a page-long passage detailing incidents in which settlers from the Itamar outposts had attacked Yanun villagers. During the appeal, the state changed its position twice. First it recanted the initial argument and claimed the Palestinians were being prevented from working their lands solely in order to protect the settlers, but subsequently it resurrected the assertion that the reason for the prohibition was also to protect the Palestinians from settlers' attacks. The Supreme Court accepted the argument that the IDF should not prevent Palestinians' access to their lands for their own protection. It ruled, conversely, however, that if the prohibition was issued in order to protect the settlers, then it was permitted. To a proportional extent.

It's amazing, I observe to Yehuda, how everything here is always so proportional.

* * *

Tirael has gone to visit some friends, so I leave the students' house and walk past the playground toward the outpost's exit. There is no one around, and all I see are two houses in the distance. It's beautiful here, with the grass and the olive trees and the golden wheat in the sunlight, and the dark green hills—a fan of colors all around, with only a soft breeze to break the silence. Standing in this spot, the outside world feels like a rumor. Then I spot Tirael walking up the path toward me.

Tirael has always had greater aspirations than just living on some outpost. The student village belongs to Kedma, an organization she founded which aims to build similar projects in other settlements, in partnership with the regional councils. She says her organization is the only one working in the settlements, although there are others that operate within the Green Line. The model is taking off: in addition to the village here on Hill 777, there is another in Ma'ale Ephraim in the Jordan Valley, where Tirael now lives, and a new one underway in the settlement of Shim'ah, in South Mount Hebron. "We have huge demand," she says. "This year we interviewed four hundred students, and ended up accepting a hundred of them."

"How is your co-operation with the councils?"

"Excellent. They're very supportive of us."

"It's hard for me to picture you fitting in at the big Yesha Council meetings."

"Do you mean the Ashkenazi-Mizrahi thing?"

"That too."

"The first place I encountered discrimination against Mizrahis was in the film department at Tel Aviv University. There were three of us black Mizrahi women there, and one of the lecturers humiliated us, and at the end of the course she decided we were the only ones who wouldn't give a presentation. But on the settlements we've been welcomed warmly. We're young, we're cool, we're not religious, and our ideology is simple: classic Zionism."

Tirael is aware of the fact that, especially these days, she represents a face the settlers would like to present to Israeli society: she's moderate, secular, Mizrahi, socially conscious. She's also eminently likeable. "Still," she continues, "when I sit at the Yesha Council meetings, all the people around me are the same color—religious Ashkenazis with moustaches. I think they understand they have to change, to present a more diverse, younger, more secular image, to arouse less antagonism."

The last person they had in mind was probably soccer legend Eli Ohana, who was handpicked by Naftali Bennett for a place on his party's list in the 2015 elections, drawing widespread criticism and the subsequent retraction of his candidacy.

"The opposition to him was more because of the soccer. People said: Can't Bennett find some Mizrahi mayor? This movement is very masculine, but less Ashkenazi. I felt more out of place as a woman than as a Mizrahi. But it's true, there is an Ashkenazi mentality, and an Ashkenazi culture, in Yesha. At school I only learned Ashkenazi history. I think it's actually here, as you see in the students' house, where we're more diverse. The real Ashkenazi exclusivity of religious Zionism is in Petah Tikva or Givat Shmuel."

These are both cities in Israel's Central Region. I wonder about Tirael's own party politics. "Do you vote for Ha'Bayit Ha'Yehudi? Do you believe in the party's diversity?"

"I vote for Ha'Bayit Ha'Yehudi and I'm a registered member." Of course, like any Tel Aviv non-profit manager, Tirael knows enough to avoid politics and so she declares that her organization is apolitical. "I didn't do any campaigning for the party. Obviously there is Ashkenazi power here, but the leadership is more inclusive, and there are already communities with a Mizrahi majority."

I think back to the candidates I met for Ha'Bayit Ha'Yehudi's primaries, none of whom were very successful in their runs. Dani Dayan from Ma'ale Shomron did not make it into the top twenty, and when Bennett offered to push him up to number seventeen (a position that still seemed realistic in early February) he left the party in a huff.[14] Sarah Eliash from Kedumim made it into the seventeenth place.

---

14 In August 2015, Dayan was appointed by Netanyahu to serve as the Israeli ambassador to Brazil, but the appointment was withdrawn after the Brazilian government balked at his settler affiliation. In 2016 he was made Consul General in New York.

It's no coincidence that Tirael's answers to political questions are laconic: she has big dreams. She wants Kedma to be an alternative to Nachala, a movement founded by long-time settler figurehead Daniella Weiss, which Tirael says just puts up a shack to make a stake on the land and disappears the next week. She wants to move to the mainstream and attain full governmental recognition. The elections next week concern her in that respect. She thinks there's a real chance that a left-wing government will be voted in, and she is worried that such a government will not support her projects, even though she emphasizes that some of the students in the villages vote for Meretz. This is not the first time in the past couple of weeks that I've talked to settlers who seem resigned to the right wing's defeat in the elections.

"How does your organization get financial backing?" I ask.

"We get money from donors in Israel and abroad, there are foundations that support us, the local authorities help, and we run a viable business model, charging the students rent."

"Most of the time you sound just like the non-profit people I know from Tel Aviv. In fact, you've imported the model to this place."

"Our group understands that the settlements are no longer about 'let's go up this mountain with a bulldozer,' but rather about asking: How do we take care of the driver's son? In recent years a lot of social-activism groups have sprung up, mostly on the left, and the settlements are lagging behind. Our work is to bring the news to Yesha—that's why we're starting a students' group for environmental issues. Even if our students end up going back to Tel Aviv, Haifa or Ashkelon, they will have had the experience of living in Yesha. That creates wide circles of influence."

"So they'll be like your ambassadors in the Central Region?"

"Yes, they'll be our ambassadors."

"And how will all this end?"

"I want to turn the lands of Judea and Samaria into a home for mainstream Israeli society. We're working hard and it's going to happen. Look around: it already is."

11

One State, Five States–as Long as There's Free Passage
Barta'a

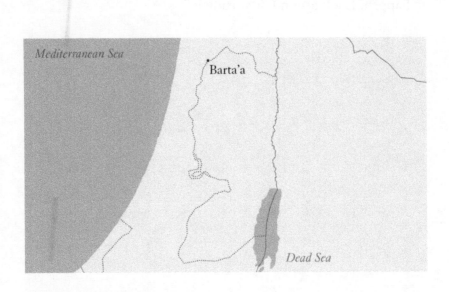

The market in Barta'a is an immensely bustling place. Cars loaded with yawning children are stuck in a long traffic jam going each way on the old road. Shop windows display clothes, food, auto accessories, toys, rugs, sneakers and electrical appliances. A cloud of smoke engulfs the kebab stand, and children peddle rings, sunglasses and electric shavers. The commotion is unavoidable, given the estimated twelve hundred businesses and more than ten thousand daily shoppers.

Yusuf Jassem, the owner of a large clothing store for Muslim women, buys his merchandise in Jordan, Dubai and Turkey. He shows me the long robes called jilbabs in an array of colors, and two kinds of hijabs—one he sells mainly to customers from around Ramallah, and another worn by women in Syria and Oman. Jassem lives in Bani Na'im, a Palestinian town near Hebron known for its educated populace. His brother is studying medicine in Germany, he tells me proudly. "In our town," he declares, "no one is interested in politics. With us, people compete over who makes more money. We have good ties with companies in China and Turkey." He used to own a shop in Hebron, but the Second Intifada destroyed his business. He considered moving to Ramallah, but says it's mostly NGOs and foreign money there, so he decided to relocate the shop to Barta'a. His income relies heavily on Israeli Palestinians, and the reality is that for West Bank merchants who want to sell to Israeli Palestinians, the Barta'a market is probably the best place.

In the middle of Barta'a, about a mile and a half east of Wadi Ara, among stone houses and a tree canopy that shuts out the sky, there is a small *wadi* (valley) full of stones, vegetation, empty bottles and other trash. Roosters can be heard crowing and cats meowing all around. Inside the *wadi*, which is not particularly wide, I stand with one foot on either side of the Green Line. The *wadi* is the border between Israel and the Palestinian Authority, and in fact this might be the only place where an Israeli citizen can enter the PA's jurisdiction without crossing a transit point or checkpoint, or seeing any warning signs. Two steps this way and you're in Palestine, two steps the other—you're in Israel. Behind the houses I can spot the wellspring that tempted the Kabha clan to settle in these parts.

It's not exactly clear when the Kabhas left the Bayt Jibrin area and made their home on a swath of land that straddles both sides of Wadi Elmiya—most likely in the mid-nineteenth century, attracted by the wellspring and the fertile land—but it is unarguable that the historical events of the past seventy years have continuously rocked their lives. In the Armistice Agreement signed in Rhodes in 1949, the village of Barta'a was split in two, with Western Barta'a remaining in Israel, and Eastern Barta'a becoming part of Jordan. That was the first time the clan was split, but in the early years it was fairly easy to move back and forth between the two parts—the presence of Jordanian and Israeli soldiers notwithstanding—until a fence was built on the dividing line after a series of violent incidents in the area. In 1956, for example, the Israeli daily *Davar* reported that shots had been fired from Jordanian Barta'a at Israeli customs officials, and in the subsequent clash four people were killed and many residents fled their homes.

The partition between the two Barta'as did not last long. After the West Bank was occupied in 1967, the village was reunited. It was now easy to move back and forth, but some significant changes had sprung up between the sides in the intervening years. Chief among them was that while the Israeli Barta'a residents had blue identity cards, those in Eastern Barta'a were living under military occupation. Moreover, Western Barta'a's economy was flourishing, unlike the former Jordanian part. In his book *The Yellow Wind*, Israeli author David Grossman depicts the tensions uncovered in the post-1967 reunification, as described by a resident of Western Barta'a, speaking of his Eastern Barta'a relatives:

> They had been all that time under oppressive Jordanian rule, and their links with the outside world had been extremely limited. Jordanian soldiers lived among them and intimidated them; they were trained to say "yes, sir" and "no, sir" and it affected their entire behavior...With them, a married son would continue to live with his father. People pay less attention to their fathers' advice among us, and every person sets out on his own.

Grossman later quotes a young man from Eastern Barta'a speaking about his relatives on the Israeli side: "They are shallow politically. They do not have a serious foundation for understanding current events and lack a proper outlook for the future...They took the shell of modern society and threw away the content."[15]

After the Oslo Accords, Eastern Barta'a was transferred to the PA, and the latest plot twist came in 2003, when the separation wall was built between Eastern Barta'a and the West Bank, effectively isolating it inside the seam zone, the buffer area between

15 Quoted from Haim Watzman's translation.

the Green Line and the wall. Although the two Barta'as were still officially one entity, the eastern part became an enclave in which 5,500 Palestinians (the majority in Eastern Barta'a and some in a few satellite villages) are residents of the PA but geographically located on the Israeli side of the wall, cut off from the West Bank. If someone in Eastern Barta'a has a heart attack and needs to reach a hospital urgently, the ambulance, which usually comes from Jenin, must get through the Barta'a/Reikhan checkpoint, in which case the patient is better off making his own way there.

This may sound eerily familiar: in some ways Eastern Barta'a—a town that is part of the PA but located on the Israeli side of the wall—is the mirror image of Ras Khamis and Kafr 'Aqab, Israeli neighborhoods on the Palestinian side of the wall. These amorphous entities typify the creativity displayed by the occupation machine since the construction of the wall. Very few people today know all these enclaves, not to mention the changing laws imposed on them, and the checkpoints and restrictions on free movement to which their residents are subjected. Splitting up the West Bank and East Jerusalem into little pieces with "unique characteristics" bolsters the occupation apparatus and aids its strategy: it foists itself onto distinct localities for which particular solutions are the only valid ones. In short, fracturing the place into a plethora of mismatched puzzle pieces means one does not have to contend with the whole puzzle—namely, the West Bank and East Jerusalem and the larger questions they raise. "You can always improvise solutions for local issues," a former official from the Ministry of Foreign Affairs told me, "sometimes even ones the Palestinians and human rights organizations are satisfied with. But to the big questions—Israel has no answers. That is now plainly clear to everyone."

* * *

The difficulties imposed on the lives of the Barta'a enclave's residents accelerated the transformation of the market—which is entirely located in Eastern Barta'a—into a lively commercial area. "Barta'a was built upon the ruins of Jenin," says a young man from Jenin who works in his father's spice shop. "After the Second Intifada and the destruction of Jenin by the IDF, the souk began to grow, and people moved their shops here to be near the Israeli Arabs." Indeed, the proximity to Wadi Ara turned out to be a good business decision. According to the estimates, roughly eighty percent of shoppers here are Israeli Palestinians, and the rest are Jews in search of a bargain. Israeli Palestinians' buying power is a cornerstone of the Palestinian economy. A recent survey found that they spend almost US$300 million a year on goods and services in the West Bank.

"How do you examine the Palestinian economy on either side of the Green Line? Are there two separate economies or is it one entity?" I ask Raja Khalidi, a Palestinian economist who served for years on the United Nations Conference on Trade and Development (UNCTAD) and in recent years has been studying various aspects of the Palestinian economy.

"The most interesting drama in recent years," he replies, "is the tightening of economic ties between the Arabs in Israel and on the West Bank. After all, the Triangle, the Galilee and the West Bank were one commercial area before 1948. They were separated for twenty years, reunified after the Israeli occupation in 1967, and separated again after the Second Intifada and the construction of the wall. Did you know that between 2000 and 2005 there were people who never left Ramallah even once? The most recent significant change occurred in 2008, when Israel began its policy of economic peace and support for Fayyad's government[16], and lifted many restrictions on movement and checkpoints mostly in the north, in Qalqilya, Nablus and Jenin. Since then we've seen a huge thronging of Israeli Palestinians to the West Bank."

"What do they buy there?"

"Mostly they spend money on services: restaurants, hotels, tourism, and also shopping in Jenin and Jericho. The trend is constantly growing. In 2013, Palestinian police recorded a million visits by Israeli Arabs to the West Bank. Without the buying power of Israeli Arabs, Jenin, for example, would turn into one of the West Bank's most impoverished communities. Eastern Barta'a is another good example. In Qalqilya, Jenin and Nablus, everyone is aware of the economic dependence on Israeli Arabs and they adapt their codes of conduct, prices and traffic arrangements accordingly. In Ramallah, by contrast, Israeli Arabs do not play an economic role."

---

16 Salam Fayyad, a moderate Palestinian politician, was prime minister of the PA from 2007 to 2013.

"Isn't there also economic movement flowing in the opposite direction?"

"Exactly, it's a two-way street. You have Israeli-Arab products from Umm al'Fahm or Nazareth—rice, labneh, et cetera—sold all over the West Bank, and there is a huge influx of agricultural laborers from the West Bank—some legal, some not—who work in Israeli-Arab-owned businesses. In the Tamra region, for example, during picking season, you'll find thousands of workers from the West Bank. But the first movement I described is more significant."

Khalidi has been promoting an interesting concept in recent years. Israel, as he sees it, is implementing an economic policy meant to benefit Jews, and he maintains that, in response, the Palestinians in both Israel and the PA, including in Jerusalem—regardless of their varying political rights—should unite under a joint economic alliance that can stand up to Israeli power. "Before 1948 there were two economies, Arab and Jewish, both of which were components of the (British) Mandate's economy. But since Israel occupied the West Bank, and to this day, there is only one economic regime—Israel's. The regulations, the currency, control over the trafficking of goods, the legal framework, all are set by Israel. Meaning, the Palestinians are all governed by the Israeli economy. The Palestinian economy, in contrast, is divided into a few regions. Israeli Arabs are ostensibly unrestricted and have access to all the potential benefits of the Israeli economy, but they are discriminated against when it comes to investment, employment and commerce."

"The West Bank is not exactly one economic region either," I point out.

"Israelis regard the West Bank as a single region, but everyone who lives there sees a few separate areas. For example, Area A, which is controlled by the PA; Area C, which is sixty percent of the West Bank's territory and is controlled by Israel; and East Jerusalem, a separate area to which the PA has no access. Gaza, of course, is a discrete and isolated zone. A merchant from Ramallah who wants to import wooden tables from Gaza is better off looking in India. And then there is Hebron, which is a sort of independent economy. You know that many Hebron merchants have opened facilities in China and do their manufacturing there. These economic areas are fairly distinct and each is subject to different Israeli regulations."

"Can the situation be changed?"

"The different areas must forge closer ties in order to build a shared economy, like the one we had here before 1948. In other words: Arab–Arab commerce. Only as one force can we build a functioning economy and maintain fairer ties with the global, powerful economy of Israel. Remember, in 1944 the Palestinians were sixty percent of the population in Palestine and the Jews were forty percent, and the distribution of capital was roughly fifty-five percent for the Jews and forty-five percent for the Arabs. Today, if you examine the Israeli economic sphere, it includes fifty-two percent Jews and forty-eight percent Arabs, including in Gaza, the West Bank and Israel. But the Palestinians' overall share in the economy is only fifteen percent. The gap must be reduced, and it isn't going to happen thanks to Israel's generosity, because Israel benefits from the separate areas. All efforts to link the Israeli and Palestinian economies have failed. The only workable notion is a joint Arab–Arab economy on both sides of the Green Line."

Here Khalidi underscores another reason for Israel's fondness for breaking up the Palestinian territory: profit, which is obtained in part by controlling the exits. Barta'a certainly represents a model for Arab–Arab trade on both sides of the Green Line, but an Israeli-Palestinian businessman I spoke with maintained that, although Barta'a works well for Palestinians from the West Bank, who enjoy the Israeli Palestinians' buying power, we must remember that the latter have far more to gain from their ties with the Israeli economy. I posited Khalidi's idea to Knesset Member Aida Touma-Suleiman, from the Joint List, a unified Arab–Israeli party that ran in the 2015 elections in an effort to overcome the higher electoral threshold enacted in 2014. "The Israeli Palestinians have coalesced into a very consumerist society, and they know that money they earn in Israel is worth far more on the West Bank—that is their main motivation for going there," she replies. "As for the idea of an Arab–Arab economy, the Palestinian economy on the West Bank is very shaky, as it is on our side. I know there is a perception that the Israeli Palestinians' situation has greatly improved, but that is a myth. Israel has increased its investment in us mostly as a response to OECD figures, which Netanyahu is obsessed with. The improvement is not dramatic."

"Palestinians on both sides of the Green Line are in fact consumers of the Israeli economy," I comment.

"That's true. The Israeli economy profits from the Palestinians as a buying force, and our purpose is not to disconnect from the Israeli economy but quite the contrary: to benefit from its power by improving industry, education and development in Palestinian society, which we are seeing some of in the IT industry. You also have to remember that changes happen suddenly on the West Bank. Products from Israel have recently been pushed aside in favor of Turkish goods, which are considered cheap yet high quality, and in fact both Palestinian-Israeli industrialists and Jewish ones lose out. On the other hand, we as consumers in the West Bank profit from this trend."

* * *

Many women are walking around the Barta'a market, mostly in small groups. They come from all around Israel. Rian, a young woman wearing a shiny leather jacket and boots, is here with her mother. She was born in Bi'ina, a small town in the north of Israel, studied psychology at the Hebrew University and works in Jerusalem. Her mother discovered the market when she was looking for clothing in preparation for her Hajj. They liked the prices and have shopped here twice a year ever since. Outside a lingerie store is a group of young mothers from Nazareth, here to buy toys for their kids and some clothes for themselves. "The prices have gone up too much recently," they grumble.

Taufiq lives in Silat al-Harithiya, near Jenin. He remembers me from the last time I was here: "You asked a lot of questions about money and I suspected you were a tax assessor." We sit in his shop sipping coffee, surrounded by bras, underwear, stockings and new nightgowns he imports from Turkey. Until 2005, Taufiq owned a business in Jenin, but after the Second Intifada fewer Israeli Palestinians went there, Jews didn't go anywhere near the town, and sales plummeted, so he started looking for a new location. He is an engineer by training, and he studied in Jordan in the late seventies. Then he worked for many years in construction in Pardes Chana, a town halfway between Tel Aviv and Haifa, but by the end of the nineties he was having trouble entering Israel and started pursuing his own business ventures. "I'm here because of the Israeli Arabs. After the collapse in Jenin, I concluded that my business had to be close to them, and they can get here without checkpoints or roadblocks."

"Do you believe in the one-state solution?"

"Do you think I care about that?" He gives me a puzzled look. "One state, five states—as long as there's free passage and the economic ties get stronger." A young man in jeans and a floral shirt wanders over to join us—he has nothing much else to do anyway. His name is Ali, and his family sells shoes in Tulkarem, a West Bank town south of Barta'a. He gazes hopefully at his empty new shoe store, as if willing it to magically fill with life. Taufiq and Ali both say business has been slow for a while. In 2007–08, Taufiq recalls, things were booming: "I made eight thousand shekels' worth of sales a day, but now I hardly get to fifteen hundred." Ali adds: "Yesterday in our three stores in Tulkarem we made eleven thousand shekels, and here in Barta'a I came out with four hundred and fifty." They both laugh: maybe the Arabs in Israel have run out of money?

In order to get to the market, shopkeepers like Taufiq, Jassem and Ali must cross at the Reikhan checkpoint, which requires special permits from the army's DCL (District Co-ordination and Liaison) allowing them to stay in the seam zone for commercial employment purposes; the authorization is valid only for the Barta'a area. If they were to leave Barta'a and make their way toward Wadi Ara, for example, they could be arrested and penalized.

We drive out of noisy, crowded Barta'a and take the road to Reikhan, a couple of miles away. The expanse around us instantly opens up to reveal rolling hills and meadows in a rainbow of colors, and there is no one in sight. We stop on the side of the road and I kneel down to touch the damp earth. Transiting between the populated areas of the West Bank, where rigid laws separate Jews from Arabs, and the unpopulated areas allows you to feel—if only for an instant—that the arbitrary hand of the law cannot reach you. It is an illusory experience. As the months have gone by on this journey, I have noticed that I do not want to reach the places I'm headed to, but would prefer to stay in the desolate areas between, where the laws are blurred.

We approach Reikhan and now there are Israeli flags hanging from the streetlamps. This large checkpoint is not operated by the IDF but by a civilian company, and it is defined as a "soft crossing," where inspections are easier and passage is faster, certainly compared to checkpoints like Kalandia. In front of the fenced passageway known as a "sleeve," taxis stop to unload passengers at all hours of the day. I join the crowd walking into the long sleeve, straggling behind young women on their way home to Tulkarem. Suddenly an armed security guard comes over and demands that I accompany him. We walk out of the sleeve and I find myself surrounded by stern-looking guards.

"Did I break the law?" I ask.

"Don't be a wise guy," one guard responds in that quiet, reserved tone that has the power to terrify because it implies that he might erupt at any moment. "You could be from Hezbollah as far as I know."

With my attempt to get through the checkpoint thwarted, I go back to the parking lot and watch people step out of their cars and hurry to the sleeve. The Palestinians' movements are more relaxed and their voices are louder here than they were at Kalandia. I meet Hussein Mukabel, also a member of the Kabha family. He lives in Eastern Barta'a and is a member of the local council; he also drives a taxi on the Reikhan–Barta'a route, and sometimes drives West Bank laborers who work in Tel Aviv or other Israeli cities. He used to do plasterwork in Hadera and Jerusalem, and he worked in a restaurant in a small Israeli town for eight years. He asks me a question: "What do people look at when they're in the sleeve? The end of the sleeve, never the sides. It takes discipline—don't knock that." I tell him I heard from an Israeli public official about a meeting between members of the

Kabha family in which they proposed that Israel annex Eastern Barta'a and unify the two parts. "Yes, it doesn't make sense for each half of the village to be under different sovereignty," he concedes, "but it won't happen, and even though there are a lot of problems in Eastern Barta'a because of the checkpoint and the distance from Jenin, we are promoting the market now and we have big plans: we want to build tall buildings."

* * *

The end of the market road curves downhill toward Western Barta'a. At the bottom of the incline it's no longer clear if the shops are in Israel or in the PA. The merchants standing around the square with buckets full of fish at their feet say we're more or less in Israel. In fact, the best evidence of our having arrived in Israel is a poster for the Joint List, still hanging two months after the elections.

In a restaurant on the main road, I sit with three high-school students, Himam and Abbas Kabha from Barta'a, and Ahmed Sharqiya from Ar'ara. They are all in the eleventh grade at the Barta'a school, majoring in biology and chemistry. Every time I ask a question, they exchange looks and prod each other to answer. I ask about the recent elections, but the only memory they seem to retain is the Prime Minister's notorious election-day rally urging his supporters to vote because "Arab voters are heading to the polling stations in droves."

"I realized that I'm a stranger here," Himam recalls.

Ahmed is more blunt: "The Prime Minister said clearly that he hates us."

"Netanyahu showed the real face of Israeli society," Abbas adds.

These boys live in Israel and are Israeli citizens, but they hardly run into Jews, except for Himam, who plays on the Barta'a soccer team, which is part of an Israeli league. "The Jewish students don't like to study with Arabs," says Ahmed, and Abbas concurs. "Studying with Jews would help me improve my language, but the Jews keep their distance. We're not interested anymore either."

I ask them about the Green Line that runs straight through Barta'a, wondering how real it is in their political imagination and daily lives. It turns out they hardly ever cross the line, and only travel to the West Bank once every few months. "In Tel Aviv, in Haifa, in Hadera," Abbas says, "there is law and order, you understand how things work. But in Tulkarem everything's a mess." Ahmed says he wasn't especially taken with Nablus, for the same reason. I ask if they meet kids from Eastern Barta'a, from the Kabha clan. They do spend time with them because they're family, they say, and some of them go to their school. They say the only difference between them is wealth. "Our parents usually have more money."

I ask what political resolution they advocate. They support one state for both peoples, but they'd be okay with two states. Any political arrangement that creates equality between Jews and Palestinians, and freedom of movement, seems reasonable to them. They are bothered by daily injustices more than the question of a final settlement. Himam's father, who is from Eastern Barta'a, obtained Israeli citizenship when he got married (marriage was a strategy employed by young people from Eastern Barta'a to move to the western side), but in 2003 the Citizenship and Entry into Israel Law was amended, and naturalization through marriage is no longer available to West Bank Palestinians who marry Israelis, which infuriates Himam. "We see things through the lens of our Palestinian identity," Ahmed says.

Ahmed's father, a long-time teacher in Barta'a, comments: "That is the difference between today's students and those in the past. Twenty years ago if you asked them about the West Bank Palestinians, they'd have said it had nothing to do with them. Since the Second Intifada everything's changed, they're more nationalist, they feel part of the Palestinian people."

I sit down with two new acquaintances: Muhand Kabha, a father of three who earned an undergraduate degree in Hebrew from the Kibbutz Seminary and teaches high school in Barta'a, and Mujira Kabha, who has a nursing degree from Haifa University and works at Hillel Yaffe Medical Center in northern Israel. They were both born in unified Barta'a after the '67 war.

"Are there people in the village who don't come from the Kabha clan?" I ask.

"You're welcome to go looking. I hear they exist," Mujira quips.

For Muhand and Mujira's generation, the First Intifada was

the formative political event, prompting questions of identity, of family versus state. They have childhood memories of being caught in the uprising of the Palestinians against the occupation.

Muhand: "In the First Intifada everything changed. You see your relatives oppressed, rubber bullets shot at them, beatings, tear gas, injuries. I remember, as a boy, the border between the two Barta'as was one of the friction points between kids from Eastern Barta'a and Israeli soldiers. We used to stand near the border but we were unsure of our place. Sometimes the boys from the other side shouted for us to join them, not to be cowards; we're all Palestinians, they'd say."

Mujira: "In that period, I had my first experience of IDF soldiers searching our house, because they suspected we were aiding the uprising. Suddenly you find bullet holes above your window."

"Was that when your identity as Israeli Palestinians was formed?"

Mujira: "Our identity was also influenced by the fact that in recent years the ties between the two sides have become much stronger. We spend more time on the West Bank. Even though Israel opposes family reunification, that doesn't prevent young men and women from Barta'a marrying someone from the other side."

Because of the amendment to the citizenship law, some moves happen in the opposite direction, as when a woman from Western Barta'a moves to live with her husband in Eastern Barta'a. Here is the testimony of Maissoun Kabha (published on the Israeli website *Ha'Oketz*), who was married in 2001: "Since I moved to live with my husband on the Palestinian side of Barta'a, things got more and more complicated. Because we lived there, I lost my health insurance. When I went to hospital to have my baby, they demanded that we pay six thousand shekels (US$1,500). It was a difficult time...Later I rented a house in Israel and lived there alone with my baby."

Mujira reiterates the claim about bidirectional movement between Western Barta'a and the West Bank: "The passage is no longer only into Israel. Lots of young people from our Barta'a travel to the West Bank to study."

Muhand: "The things Grossman wrote haven't been relevant for a long time. There are very close ties between Palestinians here and in the West Bank, the cultural and political gaps have almost disappeared, and there is also bidirectional exchange in areas like literature, film and the economy. In Eastern Barta'a today you'll find people just as educated as in Western Barta'a."

Mujira's and Muhand's depiction of the relationship between Palestinians on either side of the Green Line sounds a little idyllic, and so I ask Knesset Member Touma-Suleiman for her views. "The tension that existed after '67 was general Arab discomfort with the Israeli Palestinians," she says. "None of the Arabs, especially '48 refugees, could understand what sort of thing this was—Palestinian citizens of Israel. We ourselves didn't understand it. So they were suspicious of us. In the late eighties I went to conferences and met Palestinians from overseas and they wanted nothing to do with us, particularly with women like myself who insisted on Israeli citizenship. Today ties are much better in many realms, but less on the popular-political level."

"Why is that?"

"Alongside the fact that we were suspect, the First Intifada gave rise to a shared popular-political moment, a sense that the fight against the occupation was occurring on both sides of the Green Line. Although we did not take part in the uprising, Palestinian society in Israel mobilized to provide humanitarian and medical aid, as well as political support. Today that barely exists, everything is less political and the ties are more social, commercial, cultural."

A good example of these enhanced ties is university studies. In the Israeli media there is talk of the increasing number of Arab students at Israeli universities, but there is also a large uptick in Israeli-Palestinian students who study in the West Bank. Out of seven thousand students enrolled in 2014 at the Arab American University in Jenin, three thousand came from Israel. Majors like nursing and medicine in universities in the West Bank and Jordan are full of Arabs from Israel.

* * *

A shiny black BMW pulls up outside the restaurant and a young man hops out. "See?" Muhand laughs. "He's from Eastern Barta'a. He could buy all of us."

I tell Muhand and Mujira that Sonia Boulos, an attorney with the Association for Civil Rights in Israel, claims that eighty percent of the businesses in Eastern Barta'a shut down because of its isolated condition. Every truck bringing goods from the West Bank must pass through the checkpoint, and the result is that residents and shopkeepers from Eastern Barta'a are forced to buy products in the Barta'a market, which is expensive for them. But Muhand and Mujira disagree that the security wall dealt an economic blow to Eastern Barta'a: "The market is an Eastern Barta'a initiative, it's all on their side, and they're the only ones who profit from it. That's the main reason the economic gap has shrunk. Today people on the eastern side build big houses and do well financially, they're even putting up high-rises there."

I ask about a different issue. "There is a school of thought that one reason for the Jews' increasing racism toward Israeli Palestinians is the economic improvement of the latter. Do you think that's reasonable?"

Muhand: "Look, Mitzpeh Ilan, which is near here, was included in the country-wide plan for a national priority area, and we were left out. The number of children under the poverty line in the Arab sector is large, in most families there is still only one breadwinner, and wherever you look you see Jews enjoying privileges we can only dream of."

Mujira: "You have to remember something else about the unique characteristics of the Palestinians in Israel: after the '48 war, lots of Israeli villages took in Nakba refugees. Those people came with nothing, after suffering a huge catastrophe. Their absorption in the villages is an essential component of the Israeli Palestinians' poverty."

"The Palestinian issue was hardly addressed during the Israeli election campaign," I point out, "whereas lots of Palestinians now talk of a one-state solution. Do you support that idea?"

Mujira: "To me this talk of one state among Palestinians in the West Bank comes from frustration."

Muhand: "As early as 1994, in Oslo, the Palestinians completely caved in to the Israelis, but nothing happened. At the moment Israeli society is radicalizing to the right, Palestinian society in the West Bank is radicalizing to the left, and very few people believe in Israeli–Palestinian co-existence. One state or two states is not the right question; the question is who supports Israeli–Palestinian co-existence and who doesn't."

Mujira: "In the eighties, the Zionist left took the IDF out of Lebanon. In 1989 we made a human chain in Wadi Ara, Jews and Arabs together, to protest Rabin's bone-breaking policy. Back then it seemed the Israeli left had a conscientious role in the country and that there could be an alliance between us. We were naive."

Muhand: "Everyone here voted for the Joint List. You have to understand, our identity as Palestinians has changed. Things my grandfather gave up on because he had no choice—we will not give up on. Not lands, not education, not rights. I see the rights a Jew has, and I want the same things."

Before we part, Muhand adds, "Since the 2015 elections it's become clear: to succeed politically in Israel, you have to curse the Arabs, threaten them, and then you'll get stronger and gain support. We are the demon, all the Arabs, everywhere; the fog of Israeli liberalism has lifted and the picture is frightening."

* * *

The sky turns gray over the Reikhan checkpoint, as it did over Kalandia and Hawara. All these soft and hard checkpoints have congealed into one entity in my mind. With a mischievous spark in his eyes, Hussein Mukabel asks me: "So in the end will there be two states? Will there be peace?" Of course there will, I answer wearily: there has to be. We look at each other, blow smoke rings into the blackening sky, and burst out laughing.

12

One Day There'll Be a Very Big Noise

Jabel Mukaber and Ras al-Amud, East Jerusalem

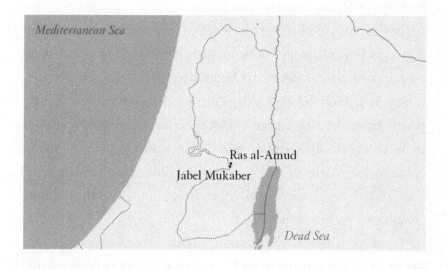

I run my hand over the smooth concrete barrier that separates Jabel Mukaber, a Palestinian neighborhood, from the Jewish neighborhood of Armon Ha'Natziv, both in Jerusalem, and throw a sideways glance at a sullen long-haired soldier trying to find shelter from the wind so he can light a cigarette. The concrete wall is about thirty feet long, and I have to resist the urge to laugh: with its artificial whiteness contrasting with the old yellowing stone around it, the barrier reminds me of a set from a low-budget American movie. It was erected last week by the police after young men from Jabel Mukaber started throwing stones and Molotov cocktails at cars throughout September and October 2015. A few locals were also involved in terrorist attacks in recent weeks, including Alaa Abu Jamal, who went on a rampage a few days ago, first plowing into people with his car, then stabbing passersby in the predominantly ultra-Orthodox neighborhood of Geula, until he was killed.

In the past year I've heard a lot about the quiet civil war being waged in Jerusalem, and in September it burst out in a deafening clamor, with daily news of stabbings, drivers running people over, stones and Molotov cocktails, raucous demonstrations. Young people from the Palestinian villages on the Israeli side, and even more so on the Palestinian side of the wall (like Kafr 'Aqab), come to Jerusalem armed with knives, intending to stab Jews. Sometimes they're successful, other times not—and they almost always end up being shot dead.

Jabel Mukaber, home to more than thirty thousand people, sits in southeast Jerusalem and is a part of the city's fabric of life. Until recently there was no checkpoint or barrier on the way to West Jerusalem: you just walked twenty steps from the edge of the neighborhood and there you were in Armon Ha'Natziv. Now the barrier is up, manned by a few bored soldiers sitting around with Israeli flags waving overhead. There is a small shopping center nearby, with a supermarket, a confectionary, a sandwich shop, a shawarma stand and a bakery. Not a single customer is visible, and the shopkeepers stay indoors. The street is empty apart from a few schoolgirls in white uniforms, who walk by.

Suddenly a red car screeches to a stop at the barrier. The soldiers stand up, there is a tense silence, and the schoolgirls skirt the bakery wall. A young Palestinian puts his head out of the car window and yells at the soldiers: "Netanyahu doesn't scare us! Let him go make trouble in Hebron, not here!" Then he speeds away. Next a shiny black Land Rover pulls up next to me. The driver is an older man in a light-blue shirt and tie, with two grinning kids in the back seat; their hair is neatly combed and parted. "I've been trying to get out of Jabel Mukaber for an hour already," he hisses desperately, "and they keep closing the roads on me and putting up new barriers. I'm driving around in a maze, I just want to get the kids home."

Yusuf, the bakery owner, a man in his fifties with his small beard neatly trimmed and black hair combed back, stands behind trays of bourekas, cakes, bread and cookies. He worked in various Jewish-owned businesses all over Jerusalem for years, until he decided to open his own place a decade ago. There are no people in the bakery, but there are lots of bees. He shows me his cash register: he's sold fifty-five shekels' worth of goods all morning. Last week he let his two employees go. "My Jewish customers won't come here. Sometimes they call and say, 'We want bread and bourekas, come meet us at the checkpoint.' Arabs don't come either: they're afraid to walk around near the soldiers. Business is down eighty percent." But even the collapse of his business is not Yusuf's biggest worry: he's afraid his children will get shot.

Two days ago his eighteen-year-old son had a run-in at the new checkpoint: "The soldier held his rifle five feet away from my boy's face and yelled at him: 'Lie on the ground or I'll shoot!' They took off all his clothes in the middle of the street—pants, shirt, everything, left him in his underwear. He lay there for half an hour." Yusuf says his son came home ashen with fear and wouldn't tell them what had happened. He didn't leave home for two days, until they started questioning him and the story came out. "I don't really feel like we live in Jerusalem anymore," Yusuf says. "Soon we'll be like those poor people in Ras Khamis and Kafr 'Aqab who got thrown outside the wall."

Two and a half miles away, in Ras al-Amud, near the Mount of Olives, it's like I'm in another world. The bakeries and auto shops are abuzz, cars fill the streets; two priests and a few fair-haired tourists walk beside us. One man brings news that a Jew was accidentally shot dead because he was suspected of being Arab, and another reports a stabbing in Beit Shemesh. All the events and names of towns—stabbings, vehicular assaults, shootings, Jerusalem, Ra'anana, Be'er Sheva—seem to meld into one vague mess. I think back to September 2000, when the Second Intifada hit my generation like a meteor, just as we were being seduced into believing we were standing at the gates of a new world. But no one is surprised this time around. It seems that everyone, both Jews and Palestinians, was expecting this but merely hoping for a reprieve, as if to say: this is the way things have always been and they can never be any different.

Across the valley, the Dome of the Rock is topped by a blue

Jerusalem autumn sky, with a meandering road dotted with tourist buses at its feet. I suddenly notice three soldiers in flak jackets, with their hands on their sub-machine rifles, examining the view together with me.

"Israeli or tourist?" one of them asks in English.

"Israeli," I reply in Hebrew.

"Then don't hang around here," he growls and promptly offers a cigarette. He points at a row of houses to our left and boasts that last night they were here on a special operation to arrest a wanted man. "We were scared to death," he admits. "The scary thing at night is you don't always know if you're looking at the guy or at his shadow."

I've come here to meet Munir, who lives in Ras al-Amud and edits the sports section in the Palestinian daily *Al-Quds*. He is an energetic, jumpy man, who seems to be looking in all directions simultaneously. Perhaps because of his constant contact with Jews, he still peppers his conversation with black humor about the occupation, which I've heard only rarely in the past year. I tell him I always envied sports journalists. "Rightly so," he says and chuckles.

"Everything looks pretty much business as usual here in Ras al-Amud, doesn't it?" I ask.

He laughs again, and tells me that a week ago he got up in the morning and discovered a new checkpoint about fifty feet from his window. His usual route to work is blocked now, and he has to drive along a series of winding roads to get out of the neighborhood: another wasted hour every day. Munir covers the

Palestinian professional soccer league. The top two teams are both from Hebron—they have money and good players—while the Jerusalem teams, like Jabel Mukaber's, are really bad. "I'm telling you, they're clueless about soccer," he laments. A car stops, and the driver calls out Munir's name and curses. Munir says the man used to work with him; he was shouting at Munir not to talk to Jews. We take a drive along the main road and stop next to a gas station, at a new barrier where soldiers check every car. Since only one vehicle is allowed through at a time, a lot of drivers give up and turn back. "Lately," Munir says, "because of all the new checkpoints that keep popping up, things have been rough. People say their morning prayers, leave home at six, and get to work at nine."

We get to a quiet street lined with large posters and small photographs of a young man wearing a suit and tie. His face is gaunt and boyish, and he looks as if he's dressed up in fancy grown-up clothes. In the background is the Temple Mount, a rifle, men with their faces covered and a Palestinian flag. The Arabic caption reads: "Jerusalem *shaheed*: Ahmed Shaaban. Fatah mourns his death.' The twenty-six-year-old Shaaban, who lived in the building we're standing in front of, was killed a week ago at the Central Bus Station in Jerusalem. According to Israeli reports, he stabbed a woman and was subsequently shot multiple times. For most people, Jews and Palestinians alike, he was just another name in the hundreds of violent incidents over the past weeks. On the steps of his apartment building, his older brother Mohammed, a tall, broad-bodied man, stands talking on the phone. He is visibly upset, waving his hands and shouting at a few boys who gather around us. They all smoke cigarettes.

"We have witnesses who say he didn't do anything. Jews and Arabs!" Mohammed calls out. "My brother was on his way to work in Modi'in, that's all. There was no knife. He got out of prison seven months ago and wanted to rebuild his life. He was supposed to get engaged this week. On the day he was killed he had a check for fifteen hundred shekels folded in his ID card, which he was going to use to buy a ring for his fiancée. You tell me—a man who wants to buy an engagement ring, would he want to die?"

According to the Israeli press, Ahmed stabbed a woman in her seventies who was sitting in the back row of a bus near the station, fled and was then shot by Border Patrol police. The woman was taken to Shaare Zedek Hospital. Mohammed and Munir show me a video clip: on a dark street, a man dressed in black shoots another man less than fifteen feet away, and immediately afterwards several people rush to the spot. I ask Mohammed if his brother stabbed someone, but instead of answering he shows me a horrific picture of Ahmed's body: his whole face is covered with blood, his body is twisted, he has bullet wounds in his chest and head.

I don't understand how Mohammed can look at that picture, but the truth is it's not surprising. In this round of violence, visual evidence plays a decisive role in inflaming the masses. Everything is on Facebook, WhatsApp and Twitter within minutes, shared by kids and young adults. Horror films of shootings and stabbings,

images of bloodied faces and slashed bodies. Every terrorist incident is accompanied by pictures, films and, not infrequently,
forgeries. People you've known your whole life send you a mes-
sage saying, "Want to see something?" and the next thing you
know you're looking at a boy's dismembered body. "This is the
new world, right?" Munir grins. "We wanted progress."

"He didn't stab anyone," Mohammed declares. "Some woman
walked past him and shouted, 'Terrorist, terrorist!' and right away
they shot loads of bullets at him. Didn't ask any questions, nothing;
he's an Arab. And let's say he did do something bad? Then you
shoot him in the foot, no? But they shot his head, his whole body.
Explain to me why they shot him so many times? I'm not saying
there aren't stabbings, but today an Arab puts his hand out to get
his ID card and they immediately shoot ten bullets into him."

Munir explains that the family of a young man who has
committed a terrorist attack will usually claim he was innocent, although they might pay a heavy price anyway: they stand
to lose jobs and pensions, and in severe cases their houses are
demolished. I ask Munir if he thinks Ahmed Shaaban was really
innocent, and he replies: "I'm a journalist, I know there are terrorist attacks. Take Muhanad Halabi, who stabbed and killed
two people in the Old City a week ago—he did it. But Ahmed
Shaaban is innocent, he didn't do anything."

In recent years Palestinians and Jews have been exposed to
completely different pieces of reality. This was evident when
every Palestinian I met in the summer of 2014 expressed disbelief
in the claim that the three Jewish boys had been kidnapped by

Hamas activists. Similarly, Israelis largely ignored the deaths of hundreds of Gazan women and children in Operation Protective Edge. Another indication was found in the Palestinians' interpretation of events: in their view, the Israeli Air Force bombing a home in Gaza and killing several children was analogous to a Palestinian shooting civilians in the middle of Tel Aviv. Over the past few months, the two worlds seem to have been completely severed from one another. Every Palestinian, man or woman, who is shot on the street, is immediately defined as a terrorist by the Israelis and an innocent bystander by the Palestinians. The truth is that there has always been a large discrepancy between the world perceived by the Palestinians and the one seen by Israelis, but in recent years it's no longer a disagreement about the narrative, about justice or lack thereof, or about the particulars of a specific case; rather, it seems that every event, every death, every incident has a Palestinian version and an Israeli one.

Mohammed is on the phone again, this time with a lawyer. His main concern at the moment is that the family is supposed to be notified later this morning as to whether they will be allowed to take possession of Ahmed's body, which has been held by Israel for a week now. "For the sake of my mother and father and the family, let us bury him. He's dead already, *khalas*, it's enough! It's been a week, let us bury him. What sort of a country holds on to a body?"

We climb up the steps to Ahmed's home and walk in through imposing double wooden doors over a glimmering tiled floor. The home is handsome and well taken care of. In the small living room, Ahmed's mother, wearing a gray dress and head-covering, sprawls on the edge of a couch near the door. Her three young daughters sit nearby, their backs erect. Meissa, the daughter closest to her, with a bob cut and a black dress, puts her arms around her mother's shoulders, as she cries and holds a picture of her son. "My son didn't do anything," she sobs, "he was a good boy, he worked in Modi'in, he didn't want to do anything bad."

Meissa backs her mother up. "The Jewish police just want to shoot and kill us, that's all. We have a tape where Jewish witnesses say Ahmed didn't do anything."

"In all the countries," the mother adds, "Jews and Arabs always lived in peace. Why don't we live in peace?"

"The gap between Jews and Arabs is deliberate," Meissa contends. "All my life I've seen it everywhere. We have a lot of Jewish Israeli friends. Here, look." She shows me Facebook messages from Jewish friends in the US and from her children's piano teacher, all expressing astonishment at the accusations against Ahmed and consoling her for his death. "This man Robert who wrote to us, he's Jewish, he lived here with us for a whole week in this apartment, together with Ahmed. We taught him Hebrew."

Mohammed says: "We have a tape recording of someone Jewish at the Central Bus Station who says the Arab they killed, my brother, didn't do anything. Nothing. Some Israeli lady yelled 'terrorist' and they shot ten bullets into him." (Ahmed Shaaban stabbed a seventy-two-year-old woman from Bnei Brak, who suffered moderate injuries. When we talked with her by phone, she asked that her name not be mentioned.)

Suddenly the mother grimaces. She fans her hands and shouts out in despair, and her daughters calm her. She flutters in their arms. It turns out she hadn't known that her son had been shot ten times until she heard what Mohammed just let slip. She'd been told there was a single bullet. Mohammed stares helplessly at his mother, who crumples on the couch and buries her face in her lap while her daughters hug her and glare at their brother. After a short silence, he shouts, "*Khalas!* Enough! You've killed us. There will never be peace between Jews and Arabs."

The sisters say maybe there will be peace one day; they have Jewish friends who want to live in peace with Arabs. But Mohammed insists it will not happen, and he tells us that after Ahmed was killed he and the third brother were fired from their jobs because they are now considered the brothers of a terrorist. "After I get the body back I'll do anything! I'm willing to die so that the man who murdered my brother will stand trial!" he yells. "My brother stood and put his hands up and shouted 'Don't shoot, don't shoot,' and they shot his whole body."

His mother tries to calm him: "Don't do anything!" she pleads. Meissa gets up to steady her brother, but he storms out and slams the door behind him. The mother straightens up and pushes her daughters away. She looks at me with red eyes. "Just give me my son's body," she says quietly, "I want to bury him in peace, without shootings, without demonstrations. I just want to bury my son."

* * *

The road next to Munir's house is blocked by four hulking blocks of concrete. The Silwan Soccer Club building is a few yards away, and next to it four soldiers stand around a small shelter. There is a large fence behind them.

"What are you doing here?" I ask the soldiers.

"Guarding the Jews' houses."

"Where?"

They point to the fence, which surrounds a crowded group of homes. I notice a few Israeli flags. This is the Jewish settlement of Silwan.

"How many Jews live here?"

"About eighty families," they say, then they apologize: they're not allowed to talk with me. They can call their officer if I'd like to speak with him.

I stand in the middle of the road between Munir's house and the Silwan settlement, together with Munir and Ohad Chemo, Channel 2's Palestinian affairs correspondent. The soldiers watch us, looking slightly bewildered.

I ask Munir and Ohad how they explain the latest outbreak of violence.

"You have to distinguish between the West Bank and Jerusalem," Ohad says. "In Jerusalem, al-Aqsa plays a major role; in the West Bank less so, I think. There are a hundred thousand unemployed college graduates on the West Bank. It's a barrel of gunpowder, you see. The frustration of educated people who are jobless led to the Arab Spring, and this protest corresponds with the Arab Spring. At the beginning of the riots, what you saw in the West Bank was mostly organized protests by students from An-Najah University in Nablus, or from Birzeit University, and the Palestinian Authority has an easier time controlling them because they have leaderships. But then it swept up unorganized people, and they were harder to confine. What we're talking about here is a discourse of human rights, a liberal discourse in many respects."

"So you think on the West Bank the story is mainly economic?"

"A while ago I met a young man from Ramallah. He said there would be major riots soon. They'll say it's al-Aqsa, they'll say it's the occupation, it's Israel, but it's all about economics. On the West Bank, for example, I don't think they're really going out to the streets because of al-Aqsa. These are secular demonstrations about human rights, demonstrations of economic anger. A lot of the Palestinian economy is centered around Ramallah, but elsewhere conditions are harsher and there is no improvement on the horizon. And there's something else: you see refugee camps rising up—Jenin, Kalandia, Balata—and they're challenging Abu Mazen's ability to govern, too. Remember that Hamas doesn't want to shoot from Gaza, but it always wants to carry out terrorist attacks in the West Bank, like the murder of the Henkins.[17] That is what preoccupies Hamas all the time."

"You're talking about Hamas, but what we're seeing is mostly

17 Eitam and Na'ama Henkin were shot to death on 1 October, 2015, when they were driving on a West Bank road with their four children.

young men with knives," I say.

Munir stresses that for young people from Jerusalem, the al-Aqsa Mosque is precisely the issue. "Remember something important: in Israel they don't talk about it and they say it's all the PA's incitement, but the truth is that in the past few years Israel has been systematically trying to change the status quo at al-Aqsa. Suddenly there are a lot more Jews around there every day, lots of right-wing elements bringing people over there, you see young Jews going up to al-Aqsa and provoking the Palestinians, you see Israeli government ministers going there. It drives the Palestinians mad when they see Israeli government ministers. For them that's the government, they don't understand that it's not exactly Netanyahu but a different party."

I recollect my visit to the Temple Mount a few months ago, when I walked beside three young Jews. At some point they stopped and shut their eyes, and the Muslims got angry and started yelling that they were secretly praying, and Jews are not allowed to pray on the Temple Mount. Then the Israeli police and the Waqf hurried the young men out of the square.

"That's exactly what I'm saying," Munir explains. "All of a sudden these things are happening there every day, young Jews praying there, and they didn't used to. This is a change that has happened in the past few years. The Palestinians don't trust Israel. They've seen for seventy years now that Israel takes away everything that used to be theirs and denies it all, it steals and plays innocent. So why shouldn't Israel also want al-Aqsa?"

"Remember that in East Jerusalem, unlike the West Bank

and Gaza, there is no local leadership," Ohad interjects. "The leaderships were systematically dismantled, so there are neighborhoods with committees or token leaders, and there are places like the Shuafat Refugee Camp or Isawiya, where there's no leadership, no real institutions, and no one who can impose anything on young people."

"Netanyahu had a pretty well-structured approach that worked well for most Israelis," I observe. "The idea was to preserve the status quo without paying any significant price, without the risks of peace or of a big war, entrenching and improving the existing state of affairs. It worked for years: economically, Israel did better than most Western countries, Netanyahu managed to fend off international condemnation, the removal of some barriers in the West Bank helped take the pressure off, in the international arena there were all the issues with Abu Mazen and the UN and the EU—but nothing very significant against Israel transpired. It also turned out that the US did not have the capacity to pressure Netanyahu on the Palestinian issue, which can be attributed to Obama's loss of interest. So Netanyahu whiled away the years without negotiating, without a peace process, all the while expanding the settlements without paying any real price. He even proved that, in contrast to the accepted wisdom of the nineties, there is no correlation between peace and growth or between occupation and growth. But now it seems that's over, doesn't it? Maybe we're actually in a new era?"

"It was always going to happen, it was simply a question of time," Munir says. "The Palestinians don't believe in any negotiations and haven't for many years. Let's look at Jerusalem as the story that really contains everything: the gap between East Jerusalem and West Jerusalem is massive. We have no infrastructure, no recreational options, no master plan, no decent jobs, nothing. It's obvious that things have to come to a head eventually, whether now or in two years, or in ten years. There'll be a different catalyst each time, but it's always the same story. Don't you see it? Look ahead: now things are violent, and in a couple of months or a year they might be quiet again, and then there'll be violence again, and it'll quieten down again, and then a little noise and then more quiet, and then a big noise. One day there'll be a very big noise. That seems to be our future, unless something dramatic happens that I cannot envision. Don't you see that?"

Phantom Time

Not long ago, I strolled along the spotless streets of Rawabi, a new Palestinian city being built near Ramallah, with Jack Nassar, the project's development manager. He is an educated young man, smartly dressed and well compensated. We walked past the impressive amphitheater, strolled through expansive parks, saw the church and the mosque, and viewed upscale three-bedroom apartments selling for US$150,000 apiece. No one lives here yet, but the city planners have already declared that Rawabi is the future. "Talking about the future," I asked Nassar, "do you support the two-state solution or a single state?"

"Both," he replied. "My father was banished from the Katamon neighborhood in Jerusalem in the '48 war. My desire is that there be peace and that I go back there one day."

I found it strange to hear him mention Katamon, where my parents and my two older brothers lived before I was born. "But the peace agreement under consideration outlines two states within the 1967 borders, more or less," I said.

"Peace for me is to go back to Katamon," he asserted. "I don't mind living under Israeli sovereignty."

"But you have a good life here in Ramallah, you have friends, a middle-class lifestyle, you're building this future Palestinian city, yet still you yearn for the old Katamon neighborhood?"

"That's true. Katamon is my family's home."

"Isn't that a little strange?" I persisted. "After all, you've never been there, Katamon is a completely different place now. How can you say that you want to live in a place you've never been to?"

"It's our home."

"This place is full of refugees, there are Jews who were refugees, whose homes were in Baghdad or Alexandria or even Vienna and they can't go back. Maybe going back is not always possible?"

"I believe with all my heart that everyone must have the right to return to his home. Jews and Arabs."

This young man—not an extremist, neither a left-winger nor a right-winger—was not particularly interested in questions of sovereignty, borders or a Palestinian state. As far as he was concerned, he could live in Israel or Palestine, as long as he went back to his father's house in Katamon. I don't know whether he would really want to go back to Katamon were he to be offered the choice. I suspect he would not—after all, his father's house no longer exists, and he admitted that his life here was fascinating. But that is not the heart of the matter: conceptually, among the Palestinians I met, the '48 war is the point of departure for every discussion of the conflict. Not by chance did former Prime Minister Ehud Barak say, after the failure of Camp David, in 2000: "I came here to talk about 1967 and Arafat spoke of 1948." That was a decisive statement, perhaps the most accurate acknowledgement Barak ever made in his political life, and it symbolized the fundamental misunderstanding between the sides.

All the known peace initiatives address the '67 occupation and view discussion of '48 as an obstacle to peace. And yet all of those initiatives have failed to achieve any sustainable solution. Why is that? Perhaps because the solution must embody a historical continuity that encompasses both these dates. It is essential to do away with the artificial disconnect between '67 and '48 and create a framework in which there is mutual acknowledgement of the decisive events that occurred in both wars. Even before presenting an outline for resolution, there must be sincere discussion about the conflict's history, about these two critical points in time, which cannot be viewed discretely.

We have already learned that past ideas for a peace accord have attempted to circumvent the fundamental chasm between the historical viewpoints, insisting instead on telling each side: "Believe whatever you want, but let's progress to a pragmatic arrangement now." Except that, as the negotiations dragged on and the years passed, and the more bloodshed and death and wars and operations and settlements we witnessed, the clearer it became that it is impossible to ignore the past or to stow '48 up in some attic, certainly when the consequences of that war are engraved on the walls of every Palestinian town, refugee camp and family home. William Morris wrote: "Men fight and lose the battle, and the thing that they fought for comes about in spite of their defeat, and when it comes it turns out not to be what they meant, and other men have to fight for what they meant under another name."

Not long ago I asked a group of Israeli leftists: Do you believe Israel owes the Palestinians reparations for the 1948 deportations? After all, they did lose tens of billions of dollars' worth of assets in today's terms. And, if so, can the extent of compensation be evaluated?

The responses to my question ranged from contempt to fury to mockery. I was unable to enter into a debate with them on this question, which they dismissed as pure fantasy. When I mentioned the reparations paid to this day by Germany to Jewish survivors of the Holocaust—and no, I am not comparing, of course—they scowled. But why? Do they deny the loss of Palestinian assets? The villages, the houses, the lands? Not exactly: they're simply programmed not to grapple with the question. They have made up their minds to push 1948 out of their political consciousness. But it's been said that "the past is still to come" (the question, a cynic would reply, is which past exactly?), and in recent years it has transpired that the fact that each side is trapped within its own '48 narrative, without recognizing the other story at all, denies the possibility of a comprehensive and probing dialogue about the fundamental questions of the Israeli–Palestinian conflict.

People asked me, during my journey, which peace plan I support. My answer was: Any agreement that changes the situation is acceptable to me. I would happily support a peace accord along the lines of the familiar model offered in the past few decades, namely two states for two peoples, but I am extremely skeptical that such a resolution could ever be viable.

I do not know if the land can still be divided. If we examine the intervening decades since the occupation of the West Bank, we will be forced to admit that any division today would be more complicated and difficult than ever before. The number of settlers has increased dramatically, to well over half a million if we include East Jerusalem; the "settlement blocs" encompass broad areas (these are not the blocs discussed at Camp David in 2000, and even then the Palestinians refused to accept the annexation that Israel demanded); and besides, it is difficult to envision a real separation between Jews and Arabs on the West Bank, and even less so in Jerusalem. All that, without even beginning to debate 1948.

There is a reason why the negotiations have become a charade that clearly cannot bring about results. Israel does not have a government that is interested in implementing any of the steps discussed, even if international pressure is turned up a little, and the reality is that Prime Minister Netanyahu spoke the truth in the 2015 election campaign when he said that he had abandoned the two-state vision, while the Palestinians on their part have despaired (justifiably) of negotiating with Israel and they pin their hopes on international entities. For many years we have been moving in the opposite direction from the two-state vision, sitting on a boat that sails further and further away from land, yet still believing that some daring initiative or formative historical moment will somehow make us reverse course and get back to where we were heading.

For years we have viewed the period of occupation and oppression as a sort of phantom time that must be traversed, a corridor we must walk down until a solution is inevitably implemented—until we end up with two states. We wanted to believe that this distinct interval of time does not epitomize the people we really are, does not reflect our nature, the portrait of our Israeli society, our morality, our army. Except that this phantom time has now stretched on for five decades—half a century—which is most of Israel's existence, and it is time to admit: the occupation is the image of our society, the image of our institutions, our army, and our image as citizens. An overwhelming majority of institutions in Israel are dedicated to the preferential treatment of Jews over non-Jews and to the elaboration of the occupation: it is a part of their programming. And now we must ask: How much longer will we live under the illusion that this is simply a phantom time that will soon end?

The year 2017 marks fifty years since the occupation. "Fifty years, it's just inconceivable," an old-time leftist activist told me with a grimace. "We honestly believed for many years that the occupation was a nightmare we'd wake up from soon." Indeed, in the seventies and eighties only a few believed that the occupation and the settlement enterprise would not just become firm facts but would set down roots and become normalized with every passing day. In the books and essays I read as a boy, it was always clear that this was a temporary aberration in Israel's history, which would soon be repaired. But the years went by and the prevailing winds in Israel changed, and today you will find many well-intentioned people here who have been defeated by the consistent reality of the occupation, who have accepted the fact that change will not occur in their lifetimes. In fact, perhaps to protect themselves from the frustration and anger, they no longer talk about the occupation and the future.

So how, after all this, do we act to bring about change? Some claim—and have been doing so for about thirty years—that we must wait for international intervention to impose the two-state solution. But to me this is a grave mistake and a false hope: the international community has disappointed the peace-supporters and done little to solve the conflict. The US has been exposed as an unreliable mediator and Europe has not stepped in to take its place. In fact, it's fair to say that we have been abandoned here, we Israelis and Palestinians, and we must solve this century-old conflict ourselves. Others claim we must view the entire expanse, as it is now and without any illusions, as one controlled by Israel, and must act accordingly to provide all the people living in it with fully equal rights. Others would counter that a single state could deteriorate into a bloody civil war, as has happened in other such amalgamations, most notably the former Yugoslavia, or into a demographic battle in which each side aspires to a majority in order to oppress the other side; this certainly seems likely when viewed in light of the current hatred and estrangement between Jews and Arabs.

There are other ideas, of course, such as "Two States One Homeland," meaning two separate states within the 1967 borders that maintain free movement between them, where settlers do not lose their homes (which would albeit be under Palestinian sovereignty), and where Jack Nassar of Rawabi could theoretically live in Katamon in Jerusalem. Each political organization presents its own model, but the truth is that in recent years, at least in the main political arena, there is no serious discussion about the future. What we see is lazy thinking, lack of courage and an avoidance of any positive vision for change. The terror of the future has paralyzed us. Seven decades into Israel's existence, the country still has no permanent borders, still encompasses territories where the sovereignty is vague and still cannot offer any viable political resolution.

What we then are forced to discover is that the most stable aspect of the past decades is the prolongation of this phantom time, the steadfastness of the status quo. If it has survived for fifty years, why not for another thirty or fifty? Some might object that the status quo will not go on, it's impossible, it can't be, no chance. Well, I heard such talk in the eighties, I've been hearing it for four decades, and I've learned to be cautious about such firm assertions. The perpetuation of the status quo (which has survived worse waves of violence than the one that began in September of 2015) is a real danger to those who do not wish to live in an apartheid state. Some claim it has already been made permanent.

Of one thing I am convinced: the separation paradigm is collapsing—geographically, demographically, politically. What political model can replace it? The answer must begin with a brave and sober grappling with the 1948 war and the Palestinian Nakba, then with the 1967 occupation, and finally with the present reality on the lands of the West Bank. In a more profound sense, we must perhaps acknowledge that the situation will not change as a result of a peace deal à la Camp David or Geneva. The problem is not one of architecture. In fact, there are lots of creative plans, some of which I have outlined in this book. What is required now is no less than a revolution in Israeli society's value system, predicated on one simple principle: in two states, in a confederation, in a single state—the Jew and the non-Jew must be equal in every sense. The Jewish-Israeli propaganda machine is dedicated to dissolving this principle, turning it into a fantasy whispered by the naive, but it is this principle—and not two states or one state—on which there can never be any compromise.

Lots of people I meet in Israel, on the West Bank and around the world, fear the moment when the conflict becomes unsolvable. Over the last couple of years I have wondered more than once: Are we already at that point and we just haven't noticed? Do we know this to be true in our hearts but are afraid to admit it? That is possible. Only history will tell. We who examine the present from street-level (and not from a mountaintop) recognize our limitations; we see the fog that always obscures our view, and we must persist in the effort to end the occupation in our lifetimes. We may discover in the coming decade whether we have the power to change this momentum, to shape our future, or if we will have to recognize that phantom time is the only time we have, and that the corridor we are walking down has no end.

The end, perhaps, goes back to the beginning: there is not much time left, and we must believe that we can achieve reconciliation between the two peoples even if the models we once believed in are no longer valid. Do we have any other option?

WITHDRAWN